IN MY MIND

From His Life with Autism, Alex Answers All Your Questions

ALEX OLINKIEWICZ

In collaboration with
Richard O'Connell, EdD

In My Mind: From His Life with Autism, Alex Answers All Your Questions

All marketing and publishing rights guaranteed to and reserved by:

FUTURE HORIZONS INC.

721 W. Abram St • Arlington, TX 76013

(800) 489-0727 (toll-free)

(817) 277-0727

(817) 277-2270 (fax)

E-mail: *info@fhautism.com*

www.fhautism.com

ISBN: 978-1935274-90-2

Welcome to Shelter Island, New York:

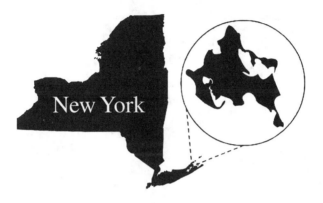

The home of Alex Olinkiewicz and the wonderful
"Shelter Islanders," who so generously contributed
to the production of this book.

This book is dedicated to all those who want to understand.

ACKNOWLEDGMENTS

Special thanks to all those who helped with this book:

James, *my dad*

Allyson, *my mom*

Kate, *my stepmom*

Don, *my stepdad*

Brittany and Kate *(my sisters)* and Chandler *(my brother)*

Paul and Claudia, *my grandparents*

Myra, *my grandmother*

Janet, *my aunt and proofreader*

Mrs Robin Anderson, *my teacher and friend*

Dr Richard O'Connell, *my friend and collaborator in this book*

Harald Olson, *my friend*

Liza Clark, *my friend*

Jordan Homer, *my typist*

Aleshia M. Taylor, *my proofreader and administrative assistant*

Andrew Payne, *my typist*

Beverly Walz, *my photographer*

Thank you to the Shelter Island Lions Club and The Shelter Island Educational Foundation, for their generous support.

EXPLANATION OF ORIGINAL BOOK COVER

IN MY MIND

A Journey Through My Life With Asperger's/Autism

ALEX OLINKIEWICZ

In Collaboration With Dr. Richard O'Connell

D id you have any trouble reading my name on the book cover? It seems to get lost in the general formatting and the color of the page. I hope you do not think it is a sloppy job. Rather, it is a meaningful ploy. It is meant to give you some indication of how the autistic mind works. For some of us with Asperger's syndrome or autism, we do not see things in the normal way. What is quite obvious to the "normal" mind may elude us.

Above the caricature of my face are a number of graphics that seem to be floating around in space. Each one is a graphic that will surface in the course of this book. They are meant to be metaphors that will help explain how my mind works. I hope you enjoy your journey through my mind and come to understand both the beauty and the confusion that make up the mind of the person with Asperger's or autism.

A Tribute to Hans Asperger (1906-1980)

The man who gave his name to "Asperger's syndrome" and who defended autistic children from Nazi eugenics

As a child, Hans Asperger appeared to have exhibited some features of the very condition named after him. Later in his professional career, Asperger called his young patients "little professors" and believed the individuals he described would be capable of exceptional achievement and original thought later in life. In a society governed by the Nazi eugenics policy of sterilizing and killing social deviants and the mentally handicapped, Asperger wrote an article in which he passionately defended the value of autistic individuals, writing:

> We are convinced, then, that autistic people have their place in the organism of the social community. They fulfill their role well, perhaps better than anyone else could, and we are talking of people who as children had the greatest difficulties and caused untold worries to their care-givers.

February 18, Hans Asperger's birthday, is now celebrated as National Asperger's Day.*

Will we no longer be designating *Asperger's syndrome* as such?

This has been a reasonable question to ask in the midst of the furor over the American Psychiatric Association's proposed changes to the way autism spectrum disorders are diagnosed—and the way this will affect the future treatment of children with the disorder.

The fifth edition of the *Diagnostic and Statistical Manual of Mental Disorders* (DSM-5)—the profession's standard diagnostic reference for mental disorders—does not contain Asperger's syndrome at all. Instead, all diagnoses of autism—of which Asperger's syndrome has been considered a subset—

---

* Adapted from Wikipedia.

have been collapsed together into one spectrum and rated in gradations from mild to severe.

Whatever the designation, Hans Asperger's name will live on for many years to come.

Foreword

Rarely does one get to read about not the causes but the mystifying effects within the mind of a young man who has the mental disorder commonly known as Asperger's syndrome—now a form of autism considered to be found at the lower end of the autism spectrum.

A unique opportunity is afforded us by Alex Olinkiewiz, the author of the very successful YouTube video, "In My Mind," which has astounded more than 1,300,000 viewers. In his book with same name, he reveals, illuminates, and describes with great insights exactly what is going on in his mind.

Not all children with Asperger's syndrome have the same symptoms. Each individual reflects a different variation of color (a spectrum) at the mild end of the rainbow (of autism). Alex's particular colors (his revelations) are incisive and give others a deeper understanding, as well as a greater feeling, of the pain and joy our fellow human beings with Asperger's experience during their journeys through life.

Many experts will tell us what Asperger's syndrome is— its causes and symptoms. Parents will describe their journey through life with their children who have Asperger's. Brothers and sisters will share their hardships in dealing with a sibling who has Asperger's. Schoolteachers, psychologists, and school administrators will tell of their experiences, their extensive efforts, their mistakes, and their coming to understand children with Asperger's syndrome.

However, few young people with Asperger's syndrome have attempted to actually analyze their experience of Asperger's syndrome within themselves—and fewer have succeeded in explaining it with the brilliancy of insight that Alex has achieved.

I find Alex's explanations throughout the book to be fascinating, along with the clarity of his analysis and the uniqueness of the metaphors that he uses to explain exactly what is going on inside his mind.

This book came about because of the success of his online video. It was his idea and his idea alone to write the book. Mutually encouraged by his devoted father and myself, a longtime personal friend, we sought a way to achieve this goal. As you will learn, Alex found school to be difficult, as well as the reading and writing process. Alex decided he would dictate his book into a digital recorder, which a typist could then transcribe.

Here is an interesting quote from Alex's YouTube video:

> What gives me a problem is reading. I can't read, and I can read. I can read a word, but I can't understand the word. The reason why is that, let's say, my mind is like a table. And the things I learn are like a puzzle piece. When I learn things through words, the puzzle pieces are put in a strand. And sooner or later, some of those pieces will fall off the edge. But if I learn through television, the picture or the puzzle fits the table. In most cases, reading is good for you and TV rots your brain, but it's the opposite for me. So, it's really hard for me to learn in school sometimes, which is why I get special attention.

Since Alex has the hardship of confusing his thoughts when writing, with the added distraction of attempting to use correct spelling and grammar, my role as editor was to interview Alex, provide topics, organize content, assist in providing transitional language for the various topics in the book, provide impetus to get the book into production, and, finally, get it published and begin the advertising process.

Since Alex dictated this book, his English will not be as polished as that of a professional writer. It is genuine. As his editor, I tried to remain faithful to his dictation and assist only when a poorly chosen word or sentence needed fixing. It is difficult when dictating to have the flow of an accomplished writer. So, expect some repetition and—at times—awkward expressions, as well as fragments of sentences, which inevitably occur in a normal conversation.

This book is a combination of an autobiography, a self-commentary on Alex's Asperger's syndrome, and a reflection on Asperger's itself. The basic structure of the book involves Alex commenting on the symptoms of Asperger's syndrome, as outlined by the National Institute of Neurological Disorders (NINDS). This is followed by how Alex has lived with his Asperger's. In this way, we were able to collate Alex's recordings into a systematic commentary on each symptom, enabling the reader to find topics of interest in the table of contents. Again, there will be times when subjects will overlap, and there may be some repetitions as Alex dictates his thoughts.

The basic format of the book is a question-and-answer structure, wherein Alex responds to various topics that arise out of a recent or past experience or topics posed by the editor. As producer, I ask Alex questions, which will appear in bold. His answers appear in plain script. Pertinent comments that Alex makes will appear in italics.

Dr. Richard O'Connell

DISCLAIMER

It should be noted that neither Alex nor Dr O'Connell are certified clinicians, and what is related in this book is Alex's story. What appears on these pages is not necessarily common to all people who have Asperger's syndrome. Individuals may have a different point of view, assessment, or explanation of symptoms or ways to deal with Asperger's syndrome. Whatever each person's orientation or training, it is hoped that all will learn from Alex's experiences, as he relates them in this book.

Introduction

If there were a cure ...

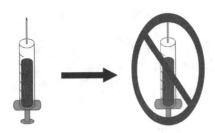

Hi! My name is Alex Olinkiewicz. I'm an adult who has a diagnosis of Asperger's syndrome. Some of you may not know what Asperger's is. There are people who have autism, and people who do not. I'm in the middle. I'm half autistic, and half not. Some people have trouble understanding the mind of an autistic person. But it's equally hard to understand the mind of a person who has Asperger's syndrome. Even though we can communicate with people, we are not fully, 100 percent capable of communicating. Since we may look or behave exactly like you do, sometimes when we act in our Asperger's way, you can't really understand us.

When you first saw the hypodermic needle at the top of the page, did you think I could possibly be a drug addict? I must say, if there was an antidote to Asperger's, I would not take it. Because I would not get rid of what makes me who I am. I just hope that because of this book, by showing you the way I learn and the way I express how I feel, that you can understand me (and those like me) much better. My hope is that you will treat people with Asperger's syndrome as equals and calmly give us more respect and treat us right. I don't want you to consider us to be odd people, who only want to get what they want. If we are finally understood, maybe we'll get a break once in a while!

Editor's note: The above is adapted from Alex's YouTube video, "In My Mind." What follows is the dialogue between Dr O'Connell and Alex.

Alex, in your YouTube video, you mentioned that if there were a cure for Asperger's, you would not want it. Can you comment on this?

There's always been a lot of speculation regarding people trying to find a cure for Asperger's syndrome. It's true that people like me go through a lot because we're misunderstood, and you have to wonder about what would happen if a cure were developed. But the answer is no, I do not want to get rid of what makes me who I am! I don't feel fully disabled. I will admit I am sometimes disabled. This is the way to put it to those who don't understand Asperger's, regarding why I have some issues. But the thing is, Asperger's is what makes me different from everybody else. Why should I always want to be like everybody else? Why should I always be just like everybody else wants me to be? I would have to completely change the way I look and act. I would not be the same anymore.

I think the real issue is that many people who do not have Asperger's syndrome don't fully understand its nature; when they look for a "cure" for it, they are not considering the full impact it has on the individual. This is likely because they see us as people who are completely disabled or ill or as people who can't do anything. But, this is not always the case. The real issue is not that we can't do things. The issue is that we perceive the world differently. It feels like this world has been built for people who are considered "normal," and it's a place that does not include everyone. We have trouble because others expect us to follow in everyone else's footsteps. Because we can't do that, others tend to think that we are the problem, instead of realizing that often, "the norm" just fails to include us.

Alex, why are you writing this book?

It started with the YouTube craze. In the past, I had developed some basic animation skills with MS Paint, on the computer. I had a talent for drawing pictures with that program. No matter how basic they were, I had the motivation to post some of my animation videos on YouTube. I had posted a couple of songs and some other experiments, and it seemed to work pretty well.

One day, shortly after I learned about my disorder, I came across something on the news. It was about a woman who had a disorder, and she made a video about it on YouTube so other people would come to understand her disorder. I said to myself, "Couldn't I make a video on YouTube? Why don't I try explaining my disorder?" So, I did some animation. I discussed my ideas with my friends and family. They liked the ideas, and my Dad was especially proud of me for doing it. And I have to say, I felt confident doing it. I wanted to try to help other people understand my disorder, and this seemed like a good motivator. I finally figured out what I should call the video. I remembered that the video I saw on the news was called, "In My Language." I decided to call my video "In My Mind."

So I created the video, and I posted it on YouTube. I was getting some good comments, and I was happy to hear positive feedback from people who said, "Thank you." Then, one day, I got a comment from a guy on YouTube who said he saw my video and wanted to do something special. I said, "Sure, anything to help. Go ahead, do something special with my video! Anything to help spread the word." And the next day, my video became a feature video on YouTube. Ever since, I've been getting hundreds of thousands of hits (1,300,000 to date) and some surprising praise for what I created.

I feel like I've found my true calling! I've found out the gift I was given. That gift is helping people understand what it's like inside the mind of someone with Asperger's. Since everyone else has such a hard time understanding it, and even though a lot of psychological books have been written on the topic, no one really understands Asperger's as well as someone who has it.

Watching my video has helped people learn so much. Consequently, people have been encouraging me to make a sequel or a documentary. Then, it struck me! I thought I should make a book version of this video, with more detail and a lot more explanations, so people can understand this disorder better. I hope to shed more light on Asperger's for many people, so they can really come to understand that it is more than a disorder. It's something that makes a person who they are. It makes them unique and helps them stand out from the rest.

In my video, I explained that I have problems reading. I can read a word, but when it comes to something really long, like a lengthy paragraph, or even a whole book, I end up losing my concentration and thoughts. My mind ends up boggling, and I can't understand it. I can read a basic sentence, and I can read a paragraph, but when it comes to anything longer than that, I lose concentration and I can't hold onto a thought about anything. In my video, I explained it like this: Imagine my mind is like a table, and each letter is represented as a puzzle piece. Take, for example, my name: Alex Olinkiewicz.

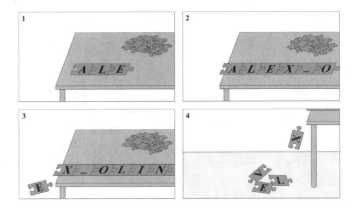

When you put the letters together, they form a strand—a nice, simple line. They're not spread out; they're lined up. However, the table is not that big. So, unfortunately, as the strand continues, the rest of the pieces from the beginning end up falling off the edge of the table. When I'm reading, all the words on the page are like this puzzle. I can't get all the pieces to match up, and I end up missing the point. However, if I learn something through a visual medium, like a movie or a television show, then those puzzle pieces can all fit into the frame.

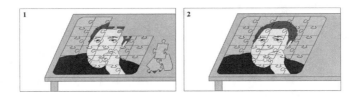

This is why I can understand things better through audio and visual methods, rather than lettered words.

Part I

My Symptoms

1

Anxiety & Panic

"May be bothered by loud noises,
lights, or strong tastes or textures."
(Adapted from the Asperger's symptoms listed by the
National Institute for Neurological Disorders [NINDS])

Alex, please explain the kind of pain you experience and your reaction to it.

I can't control every form of pain, because some of them hit me mentally. There's a difference between basic pain, like getting a cut on your wrist or your hand, and something that will send goose bumps up your spine. Those are two different types of pain. Getting punched is sort of different from the pain of getting cut. Getting punched is kind of like an insult, or there is anger behind it. I don't feel uneasy when I get a cut, but I do feel uneasy when there is an emotion behind the pain.

When I touch a certain material or a strange liquid substance, I do get mentally upset. So, I think it depends on how I react to the stimulus. That's why I call it mental pain, because it's just the feeling of fabric that bothers me—it doesn't hurt me, it doesn't harm me, and it doesn't do anything to my body like a cut does. When I get a cut, I know it's going to heal. It will be annoying, and I feel pain, but then it heals. When you feel fabric, what does it do? Nothing. It doesn't do anything to your skin. But, that specific fabric actually gives me a feeling that triggers my "mental sense." It bothers my "mental sense" more than my "physical sense."

I think that when it comes to physical pain, I can block it out by using my mind, but when it comes to mental pain, it actually comes *from* my mind. *I can't work my mind in two separate ways, by asking it to block out the discomfort inside it.* When you know you're going to get hurt, such as when you go to the dentist, you have to think of something to make you feel relaxed. For me, when I'm getting my teeth drilled, I'm mostly thinking about something I would like to do instead, which helps a bit. I still feel pain, and some of the pain is excruciating—I remember how incredibly painful a root canal was. So, I try to use different methods to help. For instance, I can squeeze two of my fingers hard to make me concentrate on my fingers, rather than on my teeth.

Those are ways I can use my mind to distract myself from the physical pain. But, when I'm hearing the noise of a pencil or touching a material that upsets me, my mind is busy working on that; it's busy flowing with those thoughts of uneasy feelings, *and I don't have a single part of my brain that's free to focus on something else to allow me to distract my thoughts.*

So how does this lead to a panic state? Well, the thing is that panic always occurs in so many different ways. When it comes to hearing noises or loud conversations, my mind will start asking itself multiple questions. I try to answer them all, and before you know it, I'm in a panic state.

For example, when I feel paint, my mind begins to ask questions. How long am I going to have this on my arm? Will this wash off easily, without leaving stains on my hands? Will I be able to shift my attention from my hands when I see stains? Will I be able to scrub the paint off easily? Will I try to prick some of my skin off to get rid of it? Will this paint actually flow down my hand? Will it give me more goose bumps? And so on. *My mind just won't stop. It will keep going crazy like this, constantly, to the point where I'm just overthinking. This is basically what leads up to having a panic attack.*

Experience 1:
Taking the Orient Ferry from New England to Shelter Island, NY

It was 2008, near Christmastime. I was 18, and I was getting ready to take the ferry home. I asked my dad if he would join me—I was carrying a lot of things and didn't want to be by myself. As we landed, I wanted to move around the lower deck and be the first to get off the boat. Dad was trying to tell me that we should just stay put and let the cars get off the ferry first. I didn't want to be on the boat anymore and was anxious to get off of it. I should have just waited.

I was carrying my laptop case, which was basically like a suitcase. I'm so fixated on my computer, I had decided to carry it in its steel case. As we were departing the ferry, I was carrying the case over my shoulder, and I also had a giant box—a Rock Band 2 box.

The problem I ran into was a deck crowded with cars. When you get down to the lower level, there really isn't any room; there are just small gaps to walk through. I always find it surprising how people are able to get out of their cars on the ferry in the first place. I even get really angry about the fact that the ferry doesn't allow much space for people to get out of their vehicles. With everything I was carrying that day, I had to be very careful. So I was moving slowly and carefully, and my dad was moving ahead, and I was almost through the cars, until I reached a silver car. I was looking around, and there was a man in the silver car, with his family. He was looking at one of my items. All of a sudden, I heard my laptop case bump up against his car. The next thing I knew, the guy slammed his hands down on the steering wheel, and the horn went off with a loud shriek—right into my ears.

Because my hands were full, I couldn't cover my ears. They were fully exposed to the loud noise.

I moved on until I reached my dad, and he was watching. The guy got out of the car and made a big fuss because my computer case had left a scratch, which was barely noticeable. He was crowding me, demanding my number and address. He was also shouting, "Hey, you're going to pay for the damages." I just kept trying to say that I was sorry, and noticing the cars waiting to get off the ferry, and the people staring. I knew they weren't looking at me—they were looking at this guy, who was making such a big deal about a little bump. Some men came up and were looking for the scratch, and they said, "We don't see anything." *I was trying to hold it in, trying to prevent myself from cowering and crying.* My dad told me to walk away for a bit. The last thing I heard was my dad talking to the guy, trying to explain my disorder. I was doing my best to hold things in, and the next thing I knew, I was in a panic state.

Later, my dad tried to cheer me up by giving me a Dr Pepper, since Dr Pepper tends to cheer me up. But even still, it was such a long way back to Shelter Island, and I couldn't get over what happened. It even became a nightmare. The upset lasted for days. Even though I had a great time that day, it felt like it all ended up being ruined because this one guy made such a big deal about my laptop tapping his car. A lot of people on the boat tried to cheer me up and tried to tell me that the guy was a jerk, and there are a lot of jerks like him. But, that still didn't change the fact that I had the loud blast of the horn in my face, as well as the guy coming up to me in a threatening manner. It really sent me into a panic.

I cried for an hour or two, and felt depressed for a few more hours. The next day, the experience still felt like a nightmare going through my body. It drained me. It took a day or two for the upset caused by the experience to fully die away. And, it comes back to me often. It still brings me to tears, just talking about it.

The problem with this experience is that I don't really feel like it was a physical pain. When I think about it, it begins to race through my brain. My body almost feels like going to sleep. It feels like there's a second layer inside my body, and that second layer is shivering and shaking. I get goose bumps. That layer in me shivers, shakes, and feels like it just won't stand still and won't relax; it keeps going crazy. My mind is still in a panic attack. It feels like it's curled up in a fetal position. I can move around, inside of me, my mind feels uneasy and crazed.

When I was crying after this experience, I couldn't think, and I couldn't figure out what to do. All my thoughts were running down my face. Even when I was better, my mind was still racing with thoughts. It was drifting away. Part of me was still hiding from reality, from what had just happened, like it was a bad dream I'd had. Every inch of my body was quivering in fear. The only thing that didn't feel strange was my outer body. *It was my insides that were all crazed up and shaking, and my outside was fine.*

Even right now, my arm feels a bit funny. It feels more like an internal feeling than an outside feeling. Maybe my body is getting better, but my insides take a longer time to heal. And even when my insides heal, they will still have marks and bruises left from the experience.

Most people would get a little annoyed and maybe get a little headache from an incident like this one. Since I was standing right in front of the car horn and was unable to cover my ears, the sound was so traumatizing to me that even right now, just explaining it, I'm tearing up. It's one of those really dark memories of mine that sometimes comes back to me when other bad things happen.

Experience 2: Hurricane Irene

On the last Sunday in August 2011, Hurricane Irene hit Long Island. At first, hearing about the hurricane was kind of interesting, because it was heading toward us. It's very rare for this to occur where I live. When I heard about it, I was also worried, because I never experienced a hurricane before, and I didn't know what it was going to be like. When I heard about it, I thought about where we should take refuge, how we should protect ourselves, and what we would need to survive. I was getting annoyed with others, because they were not making a big deal about it. I admit that I should have not made a big deal about it. But I had to be prepared anyway, because it's better to be safe than sorry.

Even though no one else seemed too worried, I tried to convince everyone where I thought we should take refuge. For example, I thought we should go to a school, but, unfortunately, the schools that are used as shelters don't open until after the storm. I learned that this was not a serious hurricane, so if they opened a school up for everyone beforehand, everyone might just crowd in there. I suggested that we try to take refuge in my dad's gas station, because it's a brick building, away from the trees. But, still, people were arguing with me about it. One of them wanted to be comfortable at home. I was thinking I wanted to be comfortable in the gas station. But is being comfortable really the point? I gave in and thought I'd stay at home, in the basement, and where everyone would take refuge. I compromised with them. We taped up my screen windows, and we got a few supplies ready for the event. I even took all of my personal items off the shelves in my room, packed them away, and stored them in my closet on a high shelf, just in case of flooding. I was prepared.

When the hurricane actually hit, I was both happy and yet annoyed at the same time. I learned from Dad that the hurricane was not as bad as predicted. It had only 65-mile-an-hour winds. The winds were very strong, but not strong enough to whisk you away, as I thought would happen. They were strong enough to tear a few branches off of a tree and knock over some very old trees that were dying, but, other than that, it wasn't really that serious. To be honest, I felt irritated that I had made such a fool of myself. Our power went out, but everything else was intact and fine.

I felt like I had prepared for the worst, and my efforts were almost all for nothing. Especially because I made such a big deal of the hurricane before it hit. *I had gone into panic mode and had upset the family.* I had prepared and argued that we should take refuge in the gas station. It made me mad that the storm wasn't that serious. In fact, everyone was able to hang out upstairs rather than down in the basement during the storm, and we were all just fine.

After the storm, the only problem I had to deal with was the lack of power. I wasn't sure I would be able to make it through the ensuing days without power. But, I had some relief. My dad told me that the gas station was hooked up to the main line, which the electric company would focus on fixing. So even if no homes got power back, at least the gas station would be one of the first places to get it. In fact, the same day the hurricane hit, the power did go back on at the gas station, and I was relieved. Even so, there were a lot of issues that came up during the aftermath of the hurricane that really got to me.

I was watching a documentary about the senses. When it comes to certain feelings, there are some things I can control, and there are some things I can't control. The documentary demonstrated that your feelings of pain come from your head, not from an actual part of your body. So when you get cut, it's actually your brain saying, "That hurts," not really your feelings. So if you shut off the part of your brain that message comes from, you won't get that feeling. Now, I know some people say, "Why don't you do that with every sense, like when you get into a room with loud noises? Just ignore it—it's not a physical pain."

The thing is, there's something different about my body when it comes to actual pain and mental pain. There's the pain that hurts you mentally, and the pain that actually hurts you physically. And the problem is I have slightly more control when it comes to physical pain than mental pain. When it comes to getting cut, it may hurt, and I may try to ease the pain a bit. Mental pain I can't handle.

Experience 3: The Flood

Recently, there was a flood in my apartment, which is in the basement of my home. And I was dispossessed. Half of my apartment flooded. Luckily, my electronics and all of my good stuff were not harmed in the flood. So, I was really happy to know we stopped the water from getting close enough to damage my stuff. However, the downside was that my dad told me my apartment needed to be vacuumed out. He said I would be able to go back down there when it dried up, "in a day."

At first I was okay, but I still felt panicky and continued overthinking, which I always do when something goes wrong. I can't help but overthink things, and I tend to panic. Soon, my father gave me more bad news. It turned out I would be upstairs for 2 weeks, because, unfortunately, the flooding was severe, and the water was dirty. So the rug had to be replaced, as well as the bottom 2 feet of sheet rock. I had to move upstairs for longer than I wanted.

This was a problem to me because I was mostly upstairs with my family, and I need to have complete control of my space. What was going through my mind was that I did not have as much privacy as I did before. I was feeling that there were things I couldn't really do without being by myself. I didn't really want to get up and bounce around the house when I thought about my stories, with my family around. I felt down.

Explain what you mean by "down," when your mood changes.

When I felt down, I felt upset, not well, and not able to think straight. When the flood happened, I couldn't take a moment to really think things out. I couldn't think about my stories I like to think about, because of what happened. When a problem happens, my mood is not in the right place for a while, until something is fixed. I can't always think straight when it comes to that. It was a terrible 2 weeks of anxiety. I was not in my comfort space.

Repetition and Rituals

"Repetitive routines or rituals."

—NINDS

"Showing an intense obsession with one or two specific, narrow subjects."

—Mayo Clinic

Alex, I'd like to talk about little habits that you have that are different from repetitious, such as introducing me every time we have a recording. Tell us about some of your habits and rituals.

Some of my habits are basic things. I prefer things to be clean. If I see things that are filthy, I always try to clean them up. Sometimes when I walk into my dad's room and I see my dad's hairbrush filled with hair, I can't help but clean it out and throw the hair in the toilet. Or, for example, when I put things on a shelf,

I always take time to even the things out; I need to be fully comfortable with they way they look. If something feels slightly off, I have to go back and try to adjust it so it's "just right." I guess you could say it's like obsessive-compulsive disorder, which is a common thing among autistic people.

For me, it seems like a slight obsessive-compulsive disorder tends to occur on some levels. It is not really serious, in my opinion. There are some things I can let go of, but there are a few things here and there that I fix up or rearrange all the time. Not all of them involve obsessive-compulsive kinds of behavior, like keeping things even or clean. Some things just make me a little uneasy. In any case, what makes these things different from "routines" is that they're not something I have to do every day to make me feel comfortable. For example, when I fix my shelf to make things look even, then they're even. I don't have to go back and redo it every single day. The only time I have to do it is when something is out of order. If someone bumped into the bookshelf or looked at a book and put it back incorrectly, then I'd probably have to fix it—but that doesn't mean I do it every day.

I don't always walk into my dad's room, see his hairbrush, and clean it up. I go to my dad's gas station quite often, and when I see that the piles of coffee cups are out of order, I must fix them. On a day when I'm not going to the gas station, however, it's not going through my mind that I have to make those cups even. No. When I happen to be there and I'm grabbing lunch, I'll do it. If I'm not going, the cups aren't going to make me feel uneasy; they're not going to break my routine.

Alex, I've heard you speak about walking into a room that is painted white and plainly decorated. What is your reaction to that type of environment, as opposed to a colorful room?

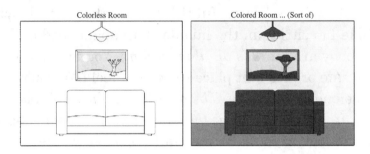

Colorless Room   Colored Room ... (Sort of)

Let's say there are two rooms. The only difference between them is that one has some colorful imagery, maybe some blue walls or some paintings. The other room is completely bland—it's white, gray, and not really decorated.

In an example like this, I think people tend to forget that your eyes can be as sensitive as your sense of touch, hearing, or smell. Not many people like to look at something slimy. Some people can't stand to look at an insect. You're not touching it—you're not smelling it—but you're seeing it, and it bothers you. For me, some things I see can bother me quite severely.

The difference between a bland room and a colorfully decorated one is this: When you look at a bland room you don't say it's gross, but it's got a different feel. I would say it feels like there's nothing there. It feels unpleasant; it's dull. It's not really a fun place to be in. You're not looking at something that makes you happy. For example, if you walked into a room, you'd probably like to see a couple of paintings or a bouquet of flowers, because it lightens up the room. When you take that away, you may feel like it's not that great of a room to be in.

Some people would feel fine about staying in that room, but I would rather have that bouquet of flowers or a few paintings to make it look like a nice, comfortable place. Since I'm more sensitive, I get *way* more uncomfortable than most people do. When I'm in that white room, it's like I'm seeing nothing. I don't see any joyful things to make me feel joyful. I feel like I'm sitting in the middle of an abandoned building, with nobody around. *It's an alone feeling.* You feel like you're not in a safe or pleasant place to be. You feel like you're somewhere no one wants to be. *The air almost always feels a lot different in a room like that than in a colorful room.* There's nothing to look at to make you smile or make you feel happy. There's no scenery.

When it comes to being in a colorful room, it's like being loaded with colors—loaded with the joy of bright things. There are fun things to look at. If I asked you to choose between sitting on a nice beach, with the sun, the ocean, and the sand, all full of different, beautiful colors, or sitting in the white room, which would you chose? I think most people would choose the beach. And I guess other people would say they could handle spending a few hours in the white room. I can only handle a minute in there. Some people might have an uncomfortable feeling being in these bland rooms, *but to me, it's more severe than for others.*

Inappropriate Behavior

"Socially and emotionally inappropriate behavior and the inability to interact successfully with peers."

—NINDS

"Displays unusual nonverbal communication, such as lack of eye contact, few facial expressions, or awkward body postures and gestures."

—Mayo Clinic

Alex, how do you describe what you call your "down phase?"

At times when I'm stressed, I can't really keep my mind focused. I mostly keep my head down. I'm usually not talkative. I also can't get my thoughts out. When I'm down, I can't concentrate. I'm in my own world, I *tend to not look in a person's eyes, and if people ask me questions, I will most likely answer with, "I don't know."* This is what I call a "down phase."

You could say that part of my body shuts off. *It's trying to rest itself from all the stress I'm feeling.* I don't want to use my strength to lift my head, my voice is lowered, I mumble when I speak, and I can't really think.

It's like when you're using your computer, and it's having lots of trouble, so you decide to turn some things off. You can lower the brightness. You turn off the Wi-Fi and anything else that may be running, just to get it to run smoothly. So, you could say that part of me is trying to ease some of the stress away. I'm not always 100 percent functional when I'm like that.

Alex, to what degree will you reveal your true self
to others?

I think people try to go overboard to hide their true selves. I
think part of the reason I learned this is that I have already
revealed my true self to everyone with my disorder in my
YouTube video. Some people actually try to hide that they're
autistic, to make themselves blend in with others.

I say, "Why shouldn't I let people think of me as different? Why should I lie about who I am? Why should I hide who
I am? Just so I could be like everyone else?" I learned that
hiding oneself doesn't work out for most people. You may have
noticed that a lot of famous people go through hard times in
their lives, because they were hiding something about themselves that finally got revealed.

I'm interesting and I have different beliefs, and I don't care
if people know it. For example, if a famous person was into
something out of the ordinary, and the paparazzi showed up
and asked how they felt about it, most people would probably
try to deny it. They would try any tactic to not talk about it
and say, "No comment." If that happened to me, I would say,
"Yeah, I'm into that stuff, so what? There are a lot of people
who are into things that are out of the ordinary. It's not affecting you; it's not affecting anyone around me, so why are you
making such a big deal about it?"

I think it's the same old story, revolving around what most
people consider "the norm." Whatever "sticks out" from the
norm is just wrong. To them, it is disturbing or just not right.
I feel like people need to learn from what's happened in the
past. African Americans were considered "out of the norm"

because of the color of their skin. So they were mistreated or misunderstood, when there was nothing really different about them otherwise. We slowly learned that we were not doing the right thing. *So we expanded our views and accepted more people. We expanded what we considered to be "the norm" and included them in it.*

Now, we just need to expand our point of view to allow everyone's personal lives in. Accept people with Asperger's syndrome into "the norm" of life. If you are not like us, you should at least respect us for who we are. Who we are is not affecting you, so don't make it seem like it's a big deal.

4

Empathy toward Others

"Socially and emotionally inappropriate behavior and the inability to interact successfully with peers."

—NINDS

"Appearing not to understand, empathize with, or be sensitive to others' feelings."

—Mayo Clinic

Can you tell me about your emotional life? When you were younger, did you respond to people? Did you sense emotion when you were young?

I would say I'm a person who tries to help out, even when I'm not even sure that what I'm saying is fully correct. A lot of people say that my choices or my thoughts seem to be helpful. But again, I still have trouble understanding what people feel. This happens often, like when I hear someone speaking and I believe I hear a slight form of anger that is enough to make me feel uneasy and upset inside.

There have been so many times I've felt that way just because there was a slight hint of anger from someone. When someone tries to tell me to stop talking for a moment or someone says, "Would you stop looking at me like that," I instantly feel that slight bit of anger, and it gets to me. I can't say I recognize people's emotions perfectly, but no one really can.

What is your reaction when you sense that people are ridiculing you? How do you pick it up? How do you sense it? How do you deal with it?

At times, I can't really tell. I think this is because not many people picked on me in school. But, I would say I was always a bit annoyed by people who questioned me on why I don't do this or why I don't do that. You could say that was a slight form of picking on me. Unfortunately, back then I didn't know how to confront it, so I said, "I just can't do it," and it always ended up not really ending well.

As I got older, however, there were a few things I picked up on. The most obvious examples of people picking on me were comments some people left about my video, and they said some really mean things. But, I expressed myself well in the video, and other people praised me about the way my video helped them. It made me realize I'm actually helping a lot of people. Why should I get upset with a bunch of people I don't even know, who ridiculed me and said some really dumb things?

So, I simply do the common-sense thing that everyone *should* do—but not a lot of people actually do—which is to just ignore them. The only time I will take any kind of action is when someone posts a disrespectful comment and continues to do so repeatedly. And then, all I really have to do is block that user from posting on my videos.

I don't try to fight back. The funny thing is, I don't seem to need to, because almost every time something like that happens, I get a positive response from other viewers, who berate the person who left the mean comment and say, "Don't beat on this kid," or "Take a look at yourself in the mirror and look at what you're saying." If people insult me about something—let them.

5

Interactions with Peers

Loneliness, Companionship, Friendship, and Personal Relationships

We are at the beach club on a fall day, and the clouds are all around us, and it's a great day to be alive. Let's talk about your feelings today, and, very briefly, tell us how you feel internally when Liza comes.

(Liza was hired by Alex's dad to be a companion and helper and to drive Alex around town. She is present during this interview.)

I don't want to talk about it—she's right here! First, when I hear Liza's coming over, I should hide under the couch and suck my thumb and stay in the fetal position in terror! I'm just kidding around ...

Well, I know I'm in luck to have a friend. Liza is one of my only friends that I hang out with. I'm out of school and I've got nothing much to do, so I run into problems here and there. I'm not fully prepared to do the next step, like most other people who graduate high school. So, I'm mostly stuck by myself. Knowing that Liza comes over to hang out with me, to help pass the time with me and hang out with me, is always a delight. It's always a great moment for me when she comes over. It sucks that she's a girl and doesn't want to get into a relationship, but I guess a friendship is okay. And, you know, it's nice to talk to someone and annoy that person with some subjects they don't care to hear about. It's also nice to listen to her problems and try to help her out. She listens to my problems. Simply put, it's always a delight when Liza comes by to ease my problems a bit and ease my stresses, and it's great to actually have a friend.

Besides the fact that she's my assistant most of the time, she has become a friend. My disorder prevents me from traveling. She is my friend because we do the usual things that most friends do. We talk, and we discuss our personal lives. We trust each other. We try to comfort each other in some ways. Sometimes she bugs me, and sometimes I bug her. I guess you could say it's just the way a regular friendship is. Just because my disorder makes me have different views and different feelings on certain things don't always make me so different from anyone else. Our basic friendship is not really so different.

LIZA: No, definitely not. And I want to say that I go to Alex to talk about my problems because he just looks at things in a different way. I need to talk to somebody nice and relaxed, and I've noticed that sometimes, Alex experiences the same things I go through. Sometimes I feel that he and I have the same problems. It's nice to know that he understands me in a lot of ways, and I try to understand him. Even though I don't go through the hard times that he does because he sees the world differently, we are still capable of relating to each other.

Alex, did you have any other friendships while in school?

Well, in some ways, yes, but not with my peers. When I was in school, I did have a friend—Mrs Anderson, my special-education teacher. I actually did develop a friendship with her, and for part of our time together, we just hung out. However, we were mostly doing schoolwork and homework. On occasion, we talked about my problems in school and dealing with teachers. It was just a basic friendship, and I owe her a lot.

I know you have experienced extreme loneliness. Do you feel that is still part of you?

Well, I still get that lonely feeling a lot. Mostly it happens when Liza is not around, and I'm stuck by myself, you know? I can't always rely on her to help me out. She tries her best, but she has other things she has to do in her own life. So, during those times, I do feel lonely. Even when I'm with Liza, I can still get that lonely feeling—that feeling about how I'm not in a relationship...an actual "lovers" relationship, not just a friendship. Liza is a big help to me in coping with this problem.

When Liza does come over, she does really relieve my loneliness. When she is here, I like talking to her and sharing what I am doing. However, she may want to go out. This can become annoying. She really wants me to do other things and get out of the house. That's a big issue with me, sometimes. Just sitting around doing the things I like to do can be a lot more fun when I'm sharing them with Liza. I enjoy having someone sitting next to me, and I can just talk to him or her. But, unfortunately, it's not always that way with Liza. She wants me to do other things with her, like going to Best Buy, GameStop, or my dad's gas station.

LIZA: I try to make Alex go everywhere with me. I even make him go to TJ Maxx with me! I know he hates that. But, he has to make the effort to have other experiences. Sometimes, I'm not even supposed to be working with Alex. But, if I'm going to certain places, I don't always want to go by myself, either.

ALEX: Another problem I have is that if Liza calls me to go out somewhere, I don't always want to go, and I get a feeling of guilt. It's just one of those things I'm never going to get used to. When I deny someone's request, I don't really know how other people feel. And I get a feeling of guilt.

As for loneliness, I still have it a lot. Ever since I left school, I've felt very lonely. I spend most of my days alone, except for Liza.

LIZA: I know how hard it is for you to get out of the house, Alex. You shouldn't feel guilty at all. We're friends. So you should feel comfortable if you say "no." I accept you the way you are. But I'm still going to ask you.

Alex, you recently acquired a new friend. Tell us about him?

Liza had to be away for a while. I was having a lot of issues, so my dad quickly got me a new friend to hang out with—Harald. Harald has similarities to Liza. He's a friend. He cares about me, I care about him, he talks to me, and I talk to him. The best way to put it is that everything I said about Liza is the same with him. The only difference is that he has a slightly different personality and behaviors than Liza does, plus a different gender.

Honestly, I think I find a Harald a little bit better than my old friend Liza when it comes to being my assistant or a person to hang out with me. He doesn't like to do things that I don't like, so I don't see him doing the things that tend to bother me. He doesn't talk on his cell phone. He does smoke, but there's never a moment where he's sitting around and he says, "Oh hey, can you pause this? I have to go outside and take a smoke." I have the same relationship with Harold as I do with Liza. He's a good friend, and I'm happy to be around him.

> Could you mention some of the positive things that Harald's helped you with?

In my conversations with Harald, he's not afraid to tell you what's right, what's wrong, and what you should be doing. He's always on time and prompt, so I always know when to expect him, which is good.

Harald's always talking about his own beliefs, which I enjoy at times, but it also gets to be a little too much. That's how he behaves, although I would say I'd like him to lower it down a bit. Sometimes it gets a little too pressuring, but then again, he does the same things that Liza does. He tries to give me advice, and he tries to help me out with his ideas, remedies, and solutions. There's not much I can say different about him, compared to Liza.

> Could you mention some of the things you think have improved in your life since Harald came?

Things have improved in the sense that now I have someone who comes by every day, and I'm not really in a panic state. I'm not fully sure if this is going to last, but, for now, everything seems to be working fine.

Problems with Nonverbal Communication

"Problems with nonverbal communication, including the restricted use of gestures, limited or inappropriate facial expressions, or a peculiar, stiff gaze."

—NINDS

"Displays unusual nonverbal communication, such as lack of eye contact, few facial expressions, or awkward body postures and gestures."

—Mayo Clinic

Do you have difficulty reading people's facial expressions?

I actually do have some problems with reading facial expressions. There have been a lot of cases when I'm looking at a person's face, I can't tell whether they're a little down or upset or lost in thought. I do understand why people with Asperger's and autism sometimes have trouble with facial expressions. Most of the time, when we look at a face, it looks like a happy one. A smile is an upturned "loop"—a basic loop. When you're sad, it's an upside-down loop (I'm representing the mouth). When you're angry, usually there's an upside down loop, with narrow half-slashes on the eyes. Those are the simple facial expressions we can understand.

And then there are those other expressions mixed in, which express other types of emotions and are hard to read. When someone is confused, they sometimes have similar facial expressions to someone who is upset or angry. There are slight differences that a lot of people like me don't always notice. There are so many symbols and expressions in the face that sometimes it's not easy to recognize. It's not like in a cartoon, which has a basic drawing for a face. A cartoon face describes what a character's outlook is—how they view things or what they feel—and it's very simple.

But the human face is a lot more complicated than that. So, sometimes the expressions can be confusing to us, in a lot of different ways. It's difficult to understand why, when someone is feeling all right, he may sometimes look like he's feeling upset. Or when someone is surprised, it could be from either shock or joy.

Can you tell when someone is fooling or joking or when they're being serious?

I can mostly tell when people are being sarcastic, because they lower their voice a bit and say it at a slower pace than their usual way. Any time I hear those clues, I always assume it means they're being sarcastic. Sometimes when they express it on their face, it is more confusing to understand. I know it's sarcasm. But not everyone who's being sarcastic gives that kind of clue.

There are other people who say things that are critical or sarcastic, and I'm not sure what they mean. What they say represents something that is not fully true, like fibbing or being evasive. I still have some issues understanding that. I will admit, I think I can sense some lies on people's faces when they are usually speaking. That's not too hard. When someone lies, they tend to stutter or pause, so it's easy to tell. But I still have trouble sometimes understanding what some people really mean. In most cases, I think I can understand pretty well.

What is your emotional reaction when you feel that someone is teasing you?

In the past, I admit that it would bother me. After I made my video "In My Mind" and showed it to the world, I realized what an amazing gift I have. *I came to realize, why should I let people bother me about who I am?* I remember that I was one of those people *who tried to hide my problems* at times. I *did* try to hide some hurtful things. But when I realized I should not let what other people think about me get in the way of being who I am, what others thought of me bothered me less. I just have to remember that even if I didn't have my disorder, there are still going to be people who would tease me and annoy me. No matter what, it's not going to really change. Everyone and anyone always gets teased or picked on by other people because it's just a common thing in human society.

Some people are jealous, or they just don't want to understand the other person. They consider that person to be an idiot. So, I came to realize that I must not let things get to me. Out of all the great praise I get on YouTube, I still get those jerks who insult me—and all I do is shrug them off. If I let them upset me, I'd be upset all the time. So why let it bother me? I just learn not to care what other people say about me.

The success of my video shows the kind of strong person I really am—what kind of gift I really have to give the world. And if I just let everyone try to prevent me from bringing out my gift, by saying I'm an idiot or something to that affect, then I wouldn't be part of the world anymore. Some people, like Albert Einstein or Leonardo da Vinci, were people who were ridiculed for their creations and their ideas. If they had let their critics get to them, they probably wouldn't have achieved what they have done for us. After I saw what I'm able to do, I should not let people get to me, because if they did, then my gift would just not be given to the world, or I wouldn't be able to use my gift.

There are many children with Asperger's syndrome who take words literally, such as, "break a leg," or "chicken fingers"—they actually think it's a chicken's finger—or "give me a hand." In growing up, did you ever misunderstand what people were saying?

When I heard "chicken fingers," I never thought they were actual fingers from chickens. But, when it comes to certain other expressions, I can misunderstand. Slang or sarcasm, or an axiom, if it's not pronounced in the right form, can cause me to misunderstand it. But, if it's said in context, I can understand an axiom or sarcasm. I can understand it perfectly fine.

Here's a slightly embarrassing story, which I don't think answers the question properly, but here it is. I remember when I was maybe three or four. My parents came home with an antique. I asked what it was. And they said it was a toilet. It was one of those "old" toilets. It didn't have a flush—it was just a piece of wood with a bucket in the middle. It was a "classic" version of an old toilet. And a while later, I had to use the bathroom. So I pulled down my pants, sat down on the antique, and did my business there.

When my parents came back, they weren't mad at me at all, but they asked why I did it. I said, "Mom, you told me it was a toilet!" So, unfortunately, yeah, I went to the bathroom on an antique toilet because my mom said it was a toilet. I think most likely, my mom should have explained it better and said, "This is a toilet, son—it's a very old, antique toilet that's not meant to be used today. When you need to use the bathroom, don't use this one." So, I think I learned that lesson. Now, every time she walks in with her fake toilet, it makes me wonder what else she could have brought home that I would have used!

Awkward And Uncoordinated Movements

"Awkward and uncoordinated motor movements."

—NINDS

"Moves clumsily, with poor coordination."

—Mayo Clinic

May have difficulty with handwriting.

Tell us why you sit differently. Why can't you sit naturally?

I sit in Indian style, which is crossing both legs—the meditation position or whatever you want to call it. Whenever I have my legs down on the floor, I lose concentration, I feel very uncomfortable, and I can't think straight. My legs are just very sensitive. They're so sensitive that they get aggravated when they're not fully bent or fully out. Either my legs are completely spread out, as if I'm lying down on a bed, or they're completely folded. They can't be halfway. *If they're halfway folded, then it feels like my senses are trying to pull them back and forth to have them fully out or fully folded. And it becomes so agitating. I can't think straight when they're out, and I lose concentration.*

This is one of the reasons I can't drive a car. When I have my legs down, I can't concentrate and I feel discomfort; I just can't handle driving with this issue. Part of the problem I have is that when I'm in very cramped areas, I have trouble finding a place to sit Indian style. Sometimes I'm forced to sit with having one leg crossed and having the other one halfway down. I still have a bit of discomfort. I tend to flinch it or move it to keep my mind occupied on the movement rather than on the sense of feeling that my leg is not being fully closed or fully bent.

I believe school may play a part in my whole Indian style thing. I'm not fully sure. It could be that when I went to school, or when I went to gym, they had us sit on the floor. They didn't have us sit in the bleachers. They had us sit down in a row, and you had to sit Indian style in that row. You couldn't have your legs out. It became the routine. I guess it came about slowly, slowly. In kindergarten, you don't normally sit in chairs; you sit on the floor to play with the toys, or you sit in the corner and listen to the teacher tell a story. When you're in kindergarten, you never really sit at a table; you're always on the floor.

I was held back in school because my mind worked so differently. Initially, my parents thought, "He's a special kid— maybe we can bring him to school a little early, and see what happens!" But I really wasn't special to my teacher—so I was held back for a second year in kindergarten. Spending those 2 years in kindergarten is where I became accustomed to sitting on the floor, and also in gym class. I guess my legs slowly adapted to find that position to be really comfortable. When I have my legs sitting normally, it's irritating.

What other aspects do you think are on your "downside"? What other impediments stop you from living a "normal" life, like other people?

Honestly, part of my "downside" is has to do with my senses. I cannot handle the feeling of certain materials—a lot of materials. I can't touch something that sticks to my skin or creates a weird reaction in my hands or my body. This doesn't apply to everything, but there are some things I just can't touch. When I went to art class, I always did my work with either a piece of paper and a ballpoint pen, or my computer. Unfortunately, almost all of the materials used in art class were things I can't handle. I can't handle pencils, because of the sound of lead rubbing against the paper. It always sent shivers down my spine. Crayons are actually all right at times, but I never fully got used to them. There's that paper-and-wax feeling on my fingers that bothers me. Crayons don't bother me too much, but still, they can be annoying.

With paint, I worry I'm going to get paint on my hands. I get too worried. And when it's stuck on my hands, I just have to get rid of the feeling. I don't like seeing the spots left behind, even if I wash my hands. The teacher says it's going to fade away, but it's still there. And it still worries me.

Markers are okay, but they can still have the same problems as paint. If I get marker on my hand, I can probably wash it off, but some of the stain will take a while to come off, and that distracts me. I can't get the annoyance out of my mind.

I can't handle the feeling of clay. It's just the texture. Some paper materials are uncomfortable, as well. I cannot handle a lot of art materials. That's why usually a pen and paper or the computer works the best.

On a computer, you can color and make all the designs you want, and the only thing you need is the mouse, which is nice and comfortable to hold. It's very basic, nothing gets on your hands, and you can fiddle around and create as much detail as you want. It just works well for me. Drawing with ballpoint pens always works fine for me too, although I'm a lousy artist. People praised me for my art in school, but to be honest, I don't know. Were they praising me to make me feel good, or because my work was good? I thought it was just because I seemed to make better shapes, especially when working on the computer.

Would you just reflect on the way you walk, sit, and run?

I walk pretty naturally in some ways. I may not walk perfectly, like everyone else; I'm not sure what is considered the "perfect walk," although sometimes when I'm bored, I make weird "gesture walks." When I was a kid, my parents and my friends and family would complain every time I got up. They said I was walking on my toes. I think I know the reason. It's because when most people sit, or when they're sleeping, their feet are facing perfectly up.

However, since I sit Indian-style, and because of how I sleep, my feet face downward most often. It's like a tipsy-toe pose, or a ballerina pose. I think the real issue is that in the morning, when I'm waking up, my feet are in that position. They're adjusting themselves—so for a while I'll be up on my tippy-toes until they slowly flatten out and I'm fully on my feet. So, most of the time, my feet are in a different position than everyone else's feet. So when I get out of bed, my feet are stiff for a while, before they slowly ease themselves back into the normal way I walk. I don't really keep my feet straight. I never keep them facing forward. My feet always tend to be spread out like a V shape when I stand. I'm not really sure about the cause; it could be a result of the way I sit.

When it comes to sitting normally, most people's feet are pointing forward and acting normally. When I sit Indian-style, my feet are twisted or turned or are dangling, so maybe my feet are just used to that. I can't jump. I can barely jump. I can jump like half a foot. I'm not very fit. I'm a little over-weight—not too overweight, but I'm carrying a few extra pounds, which I'm all right with for now. I'm not an over-weight, obese person. I'm trying my best to improve myself.

Even if I'm perfectly fit, I have trouble with running. In school, I always had trouble with running. For some reason, my body can't handle running. Because of the way my body feels while running, I can't handle it. I get a chest pain every time I do it. In medical terms, there's probably a more medical explanation for that. All I know is that every time I run, I have a strong pain in my chest. Other people probably get it too, but they're probably better able to handle it. I can't. So, every time I was supposed to be running, the coach allowed me to just walk. In school, it was annoying because I heard people trying to cheer me on while I was walking, or the coach would tell me to pick up my pace, but I know I can't do that. I'm not able to run.

Alex, describe, "I can't deal with it." What do you mean by that? What are the physical and mental aspects of that statement?

When I say this, it's because I'm feeling irritation or pain that I don't want to feel every day or every moment. For example, if the sound of someone scratching her nails across a chalkboard irritates you, you don't want to hear that every day. You might try to handle it for a day or two, but when you start hearing it almost every day, you just want it to stop. It becomes like torture. You will try to handle the torturing, but after the umpteen-billionth time of doing it, it's going to break you. And I guess that's what happens to me. Certain things "break me" quicker than they would for most people, and that's why I can't stand it.

It's the same explanation for why, when I was a kid, I could stand going to the beach or getting on an airplane. In the past, I would try to get used to it. But as I did it so many times, it became a torment, and I couldn't stand doing it anymore. People have asked me, "You were able to do this, why don't you do it anymore? Tell me the reason why." The reason is that at first, it was all right, but now, the irritation it brings me outweighs any benefit. Every pain that came from it has built up in my body, and it has reached its limit, so every time I do that same task again, it's not going to fit into that "handle container." It's going to overflow all the time. That particular activity just reached its limit for me to be able to handle it.

It's the same thing with certain foods. I have no problem eating almost the same thing every day. I eat pasta, pizza, and the same cereal every day. Those are the foods I love, and there is barely anything about them that bothers me. But when it comes to something like pancakes, which I enjoyed as a kid, they are problematic. When I used to eat them, there were always problems with them. If they were burnt, I didn't like them, and if they were cooked too lightly, they were doughy. Pancakes went away; they were not my favorite food. And, unfortunately, my dad made pancakes every day, because everyone else loved them. So in the end, every day that I ate a pancake because my dad made them, I realized that I really hate eating them. All the things that bother me about pancakes outweigh what I used to like about them. And that's the same way it goes for a lot of things. If there was ever something that I found enjoyable, but it had a downside to it, sooner or later, that downside could be enough to outweigh what I liked, to the point where I just couldn't do it anymore.

Unresponsiveness

"May approach other people but
will make normal conversation
impossible because of inappropriate
or eccentric behavior or by wanting
only to talk about a singular interest."

—NINDS

Chapter 8

How do you interact with people?

I have trouble interacting with people. Everyone says I'm very social and I'm able to talk very well compared with other people who have autism or Asperger's. They have trouble communicating with people a lot, and I understand why. Even though I can converse well, and I'm able to explain things well, I still have trouble interacting with people. I can't always understand their thoughts and opinions; I can't always understand what they're trying to say. Sometimes, someone will say, "Hey, can you just get the box of bread over there on the counter?" You might see me looking around, almost like I'm blind, even though it's right in front of me. I don't understand what I am doing wrong.

Sometimes I get confused, even though whatever is happening is not too hard. Even sometimes I don't understand people's reactions to things. Here's a good example. I was waiting for my companion Liza. She went to grab the mail. I was sitting in the car with Liza, and she was looking at the mail. And I really wanted to just get home, but I wasn't arguing with her—I was just sitting there. And I was tapping my leg because I wasn't sitting Indian style (as is my custom). And she says, "Would you just stop with shuffling your feet? I'm not taking forever; I'm just checking my mail." We almost got into a bit of an argument, and part of the reason why is because I don't know what goes through her mind fully, but I felt like she had just yelled at me because she felt angry. And she didn't physically yell—it's just the way her voice sounds. I could say that I see a different form of expression, which, in my mind, I determine to be the wrong thing.

For instance, when I hear Liza's voice, her voice has sort of a natural talk form, but when I feel like she says something in anger, she has a longer tone. Her words extend a little bit longer than usual. Her eyes sort of roll a tiny bit, and her voice rises slightly. She finds it no different from her regular voice. I find it so different; I find it to be a form of anger, which I see as a sign that she's mad at me. When I try to talk to her and explain it, she doesn't want to hear it, or she doesn't want to hear my explanation and thinks I'm trying to make her the bad guy. But I don't understand what I'm doing wrong.

I have what some people call a "recurring bad habit." I always need to hear a reply from someone. I can't just predict that they understand what I'm saying. Like when I'm talking to my brother about a topic and I don't hear a reply, I always have to instantly say, "You know what I mean?" or "You got it?" I can't just believe he heard me, even though he's right next to me and he's heard me the whole time. I have to get that little "uh-huh" or nod of the head, because I can't accept the other person sitting in silence. I have to know that they heard me. So, constantly, because not a lot of people reply, I always have to say, "You know what I mean?" or "You get it?" or, "I hope you got it?" or "Understand?" It's a recurring thing with me. I guess when most people talk to someone, they don't need a reply back; they can just tell right away from a facial expression whether the other person heard them—but I can't. I need to hear a reply. Every time someone does not respond, it frustrates me. I need a reply to know that I am understood.

Part II

My Experiences

9

My Asperger's

Alex, how do you see yourself?

I'm like a fictional character you see in a lot of movies, a "young child lost in a man's body." There are a lot of films and cartoons that have this kind of character. Like Pee Wee Herman, if you look at how he behaves. Or how the adults act in those young, preschool kids' shows, like the guy from "Blue's Clues," or perhaps the parents in "Dora the Explorer."

I think many adults don't understand how I am. For example, I like to watch cartoons. I know that there are a lot of people around my age who also watch cartoons, but they're mostly cartoons more geared toward adults. Or, adults watch cartoons with younger kids or as a family thing. If you're babysitting younger kids, they're going to want to watch cartoons, and you might sit down and watch with them. You may even enjoy it, but you won't make an effort to watch cartoons again unless the child does. But, I continue to watch them because of my childlike interests.

There's also the fact that I sometimes get upset over the littlest things, and I sometimes need to call my dad when something goes wrong. I go through a lot of these episodes. In many
ways, I am still like a child. I still react to many things that
affect children. I even cry over the littlest things sometimes! I
feel like I'm basically a child living in a grown man's body.

> You've experienced many events and happenings in your
> life that you've had to deal with. Some were happy, and
> some were sad. But as you grew up, you learned a lot.
> What advice would you give to children and young adults
> on how to deal with having Asperger's?

First, you have to find a solution to help relieve your problems. If you have any forms of stress or crazy reactions in your
life, find a solution on how to help ease those away. You won't
always be able to prevent them from happening, but, if you
have something that will help calm you down afterward, you
might be able to relieve your stress. It's best to do that. When
I get upset, I always have a Dr Pepper, play a video game, and
watch TV. If I don't do that, I continue to stress out too much.
If you have something that helps ease away the tension, it's
always best to do it. This helps decrease the stress before it
gets worse.

The second piece of advice I would give to most people
and especially to parents is that everyone has to stop blaming themselves when it comes to this disorder. When dealing
with the complications of having this disorder, I constantly
see people blaming the disorder or even putting the blame on
themselves. I even find myself doing this. But, the problem

doesn't always come from you. It comes from how society has been made. Society has built a world that has been set specifically for people who live "in the norm." We're not "in the norm." It feels like the world wasn't built for us. It feels like it was built for the general population that is free of this disorder. We experience these complications and blame ourselves, but the real problem is that since other people don't understand us, they cannot try to fix the world so it fits everyone.

In the past, when people were handicapped, they couldn't do a lot of things. People who couldn't use their legs could not play sports, they couldn't go up flights of stairs into buildings, and they couldn't drive. But, if you look now, that problem has been greatly lessened. We have elevators. We have wheelchair ramps. We have cars with mechanisms that allow people to drive without using their legs. We even have handicapped parking, so it's easier for disabled individuals to get out of their vehicles. Sports have been modified that even people in wheelchairs can play. These days, you might come across a lot of basketball players in wheelchairs. They play pretty well, despite the fact that they're not using their legs. The same thing goes for most people who have a physical disability—in many ways, the world has been remade to accommodate them.

The real issue with people with autism is that since we don't have a physical disability that people can see, they don't notice that we need a helping hand. We do not need crutches, guide dogs, or wheelchairs, but we still require things that will help us help us be able to handle this world. Since people can't see that we have a problem, they think there must not be anything wrong with us at all. So, stop blaming yourself, and know that the real issue is that the world around us needs to adjust so that everyone (including us) is able to handle it.

You were talking about how the world regards Asperger's syndrome. You said it doesn't make accommodations for people with Asperger's because they can't see a physical disability. Neurologists tell us it's a neurological problem, that some of the wires in a person's brain are disconnected or reconnected incorrectly. Would you comment on that concept?

There's still a debate on what it really is. I would ask, "How do you know that is the way that brains are always supposed to develop?" They study the brain; they know what a "normal" brain would look like. So when they see a person with an "Asperger's brain," they say it's mis-wired or charged differently. But, how do you know that brains are meant to come out that way? We're humans. We're not something that comes out of a conveyor belt and has to be a perfect match to everything and everyone else. It's a debatable thing. There are people who have disorders that seem much worse, and have similarities to autism, so it seems more like a disease compared to someone who doesn't have it. If you were born with a brain that works differently than others, is it a big problem?

You've already seen people with Asperger's that seem to have a calculator in their minds. So you think their brains are messed up, because they're a human calculator? I don't think so. I think we're all born with a brain that's wired differently. Other people may have the "common" set up, but there are people, like me, who are born with different wiring. We're almost an experiment of what the next human might become. Part of my belief is that maybe the real reason we may have

these disorders, and why our brain is changing, is because
we're onto the next step of what evolution is becoming.

Evolution happens constantly. Millions of years of evolution have changed what we looked like, which was mostly like
apes, to what we are now. And what develops is what makes
us work. For a certain animal, it develops its camouflage, and
throughout evolution, its camouflage improves its ability to
survive. For instance, there are certain birds that fly only
small distances, and their wings evolve to improve their flight.
They can fly higher and farther.

How do we improve our minds? Remember, evolution is
not perfect. You don't get born with a superior intelligence. It
slowly emerges with slight differences that might not work.
But, slowly, over hundreds of years, it may appear more and
more superior because the brain is evolving to a different level.
We might not understand why it may be evolving that way, but
maybe that is the reason our brains are slightly mis-wired or
different than others. It's slightly changing for the next stage
of evolution for humans.

What you just theorized on is a personal theory. What
are your comments on this?

What I was trying to say is that it is a theory. But when I see
a lot of evidence of things improving throughout time, I think
what other scientists say; evolution doesn't happen in a year. It
happens over millions of years. It always has to slowly evolve.
And one thing's for sure—when it slowly evolves, it does seem
to be unnatural. When we were just apes, walking on two legs
and still hairy, after a few hundred years, some started to

have less hair and behave differently. Those people were considered odd and strange, and nobody understood them. Then, slowly, more of them were born the exact same way. Until, over time, almost all of them were born that way. Those in "the norm" think that differences are weird, but, again, growth and changes are taking place. There have been theorists who talk about why more and more people are being born with autism.

People are asking if it's a result of our vast amount of technology or uses of certain chemicals and drugs. No. I think this is something that's slowly occurring. More and more people are being born autistic because it's possible that more and more of us are being part of an evolution that involves having a different brain. It doesn't mean that because we're born with this kind of brain, we are superior to everyone else. Our evolution cycle is trying a new thing with us and seeing if it might work.

Your theory on evolution concerning Asperger's syndrome is very interesting. So, how does it feel to be a part of it?

I'm not sure. I could say that it's maybe a good thing or a bad thing to be part of it. On the one hand, you feel like an outcast in relation to everyone else. You feel so different from everyone else. But, you have to think that maybe it's just because I'm one of those people who's taking the next step in the new form of life. I can say I'm happy for what kind of person I am. Sure, it can be really uncomfortable, considering how some people feel about me. But, I like who I am. If having Asperger's is a sign that I'm part of the next step in evolution, then I'm happy being that next step.

On the way home from the gas station this morning, I was very upset that there was a radio ad for an autism awareness walk. But they started the whole ad by saying that every 15 or 20 seconds, a family is devastated by finding out that their child has autism or Asperger's. I was very upset about that.

In some ways, I find it offensive. But, I have to remember one thing: Not a lot of parents understand their kids' minds. They don't understand the mind of an autistic person yet. And because of this, when they look at it, they think it's more of a disease, or a big disability. So when parents hear this, they don't know what to think. They think their kids are ill; they think their kids will be unable to do things in real life; they don't know how to take care of them. And this is a definite reason why I'm making this book, because it will help to show parents that there's nothing wrong with your kid. Autism is not a disability. Yes, there are things that we have trouble doing, but remember—what we're capable of doing is something that everyone else may have a hard time doing.

We've had so many conversations about autism and what goes on in your mind, and that you see it as a "gift." Can you speak about that?

People in our society are becoming more highly sensitive to things. Twenty, 30, and 40 years ago, people didn't truly understand autism. It is starting to become more understood with the whole computer generation. Are our minds advancing and moving on? *Autism* is the name they're giving to hyper-sensitive advancement.

Yet, with all the advancement we've attained in understanding autism, I always feel devastated to hear people speak about autism and not truly understand what it is like for parents to experience it with their child. When I learned about what other people have gone through, I realized that it is a misunderstanding. It's just what it is. People don't understand it yet. When they see it, they think there's something *wrong* with the child. Once they read this book or see my video, I hope they will understand. Maybe they'll question themselves. They'll say, "What have I been doing? I've been trying to get rid of the way my child is—how he is happy within." He or she doesn't need to do the same things and behave like everyone else. He's fine the way he is. Don't hurt the child by trying to make him something he's not.

Alex, you have just spoken of your special gifts. How have they manifested in you?

Well, I like to compare our brains to a pie chart. All human beings have various gifts or abilities that make up the pie. A person who isn't autistic has perhaps 15 percent of his pie devoted to social skills, while someone who is autistic has perhaps 3 or 4 percent of his pie devoted to social skills. I am very social and incisive in my thinking, which is unusual for people who have Asperger's.

However, the problem with my pie chart (brain) is that because I have such good skills at communicating, as well as incisive thinking, other important aspects of my brain are crowded out or limited, such as in having feelings of empathy or a sense of appropriateness, as I mention throughout this book. You see this in people with Asperger's who have extraordinary gifts.

In the mind of someone who has Asperger's or autism, there are different kinds of worlds. Would you describe to us your world, your reality in a sense? And why you're in both worlds.

Anyone who has my type of disorder is usually in his own world. Some people live in their world all the time, and some people coincide with both worlds: reality and the other world. There are a lot of reasons why we do this. I'll explain my world.

I come up with magical, mystical stories. I come up with stories for horror; I come up with stories for mysteries; I come up with video game ideas. I come up with an action show in a fantasy world. And what I do is I act out them out as one of the characters. I act out what the television show would look like. Or how the game plays out—what you may see, or how the characters feel. I move around and talk to myself, I speak out my characters' voices; I speak out their emotions and speak out their thoughts—not my own. I create these imaginary worlds and write them down for my stories. I'm not simply sitting back and keeping them in my head. I'm putting myself into their world.

Would you speak about little children in their make-believe world and your comparison?

People ask why I talk to myself. Why are autistic people always in their own world? Why do we behave like we're in our own world? It goes back to the way everyone was when they were a child. Think about this. Think back to when you were about 3 or 5 years old. What were the things you did when you were a child of that age? Some of you had an imaginary friend. Some tended to have tea parties with their dolls; some pretended to be pirates or pretended they were in an adventure story. When you were a kid, you were creating your own world. You knew that you were in it. You felt like you were playing out the real thing.

So when a kid is playing tea party, even though there's no tea in the cups, there's no cake, and the dolls can't move, she feels like she is in that world. She *knows* she is in that world. Everyone has her own world when she is a child. As we grow up, almost everyone abandons that world. We suddenly enter "reality." However, a lot of people with my disorder, and probably some others, never left their childhood world. I never abandoned my world. My fantasy characters are still with me, even though I'm now 21 years old, and they'll stay with me until the day I die. Everyone else has abandoned that world, abandoned that imaginary friend, and abandoned that tea party— but I haven't abandoned mine. That's why we live in our own worlds—because we just didn't leave them.

When do you think is the best time to inform people, friends, or your class about your Asperger's syndrome?

I believe it must be right off the bat. I'm not talking about when a baby is born or when he's trying to speak. But, when a child reaches the age when he can understand a few things, like when he is ready to go to school, then I think children should learn about their disorder right away. I think the problem, when it comes to parents, is that they don't know when it's a proper time to tell their child about it. And there are a few reasons why. If you tell your kid he has a disorder, he's always going to have that feeling of guilt. If something happens to your kid, he's always going to blame it on himself or believe it's his fault he has this disorder. Or, what if the kid takes advantage of his disorder? If a teacher asks him to redo his homework, he might say, "I can't." "Why not?" "Because I have Asperger's syndrome." I don't know that a child will understand what he has and what it means.

Like I said, there were times where I said those things, not because it was an excuse, but because it was the only explanation I had. As an example, there are times where some kids are going to be unaware. And I'm talking about kids who are 8 or 10 years old—they're going to make a few social mistakes. They might try to take advantage of it by claiming they have Asperger's. They're not really aware how their Asperger's affects them. That's a bad thing, but that's what they're doing. But the main problem is that parents need to realize that if they don't educate their kids about their disorder, and if schools don't address it at an early age, the kid will become an outcast—even at a young age. He will have more trouble hanging out with friends, since kids don't understand him. They will feel more distance toward him. If kids don't understand, they distance themselves. "Look at that guy, he just doesn't get it. Why does he act that way?"

And also, when the kid has to do something odd, and everyone else has to do something else and he has to sit out, the kids in his class think, "Why does he get away with sitting things out? Why does he get to sit out, and we still have to do the work?" Unfortunately, since parents don't always allow teachers to try to explain the kid's problems, other kids get jealous and maybe even angry. So, in fact, they could actually end up picking on the kid, just because the teachers or parents don't explain his issues to the class and try to help his peers understand that the teacher and the child's parents are just trying to help the kid cope with everyday life.

When it comes to most parents, it seems like they feel there is a "proper age" when they should talk to their children about right and wrong. And I think what we have to remember is, maybe we should not always concentrate on a child's age. Just because he's young doesn't mean he can't understand. Maybe it might be more challenging for parents because kids with Asperger's still have more to learn and experience. But, that doesn't mean we should wait for him to get older before we educate him. When he seems capable of knowing or understanding what's going on, I think it's always proper to help him understand. There's never really a "good time" to explain things to him. The best time really is right from the start. In the end, you might have some hard moments here and there, but, once again, if you don't talk to your child and help him understand his autism, he might end up with worse problems. If you keep hiding the real truth from him, it is more destructive in the end. I think it's about not only admitting the truth to your children, but also helping them to be true to themselves.

Sometimes people don't want to admit the truth to themselves. Like I said, throw out the parenting handbook and try to really figure it out yourself. You should ignore any advice that says, "wait until they're older before you tell them." Talking about autism and Asperger's is not like trying to explain sex to your kid. It's not like that at all. It's helping them understand who they are. It's like giving the following explanation: "This is your friend—she's a girl. You should treat her equally, just as you would treat as a boy. Just because she's a girl doesn't mean she can't do everything a boy can." Usually, parents and teachers try to teach children from a young age that you should treat each other equally. And I think it's the same when it comes to autism and Asperger's, because it's the same principle. It's the right thing to do.

My Frustrations

Loud disturbing noises, and distasteful smells and textures

Well, in some ways a great deal of noise, especially loud noises, tend to irritate my mind.

I know many people can't stand the noise of fingernails scratching on a chalkboard. And, I cannot handle what other people can.

My mind goes crazy; everything is bothering my mind at once. And I want to get away from that noise as fast as I can. So, yeah, I start feeling panicky and uncomfortable.

That happened even when I was in school every day. No matter which grade I was in. I was always hearing my classmates having loud conversations, which were quite disturbing. I remember feeling that way in kindergarten.

Describe how you enjoy some things, but things of a similar nature may annoy you.

I'm going to use a new metaphor to represent this. Let's say my senses, and how I react to my senses, are like *a dream catcher.*

Now, we all know, the good dreams, the stuff I like, the type of music I enjoy, the sounds that soothe me, the things that taste good—these things just flow through the dream catcher. Good dreams will flow right through. Now, what is the purpose of the dream catcher? It is to capture bad dreams. So, bad dreams are those things that I don't like: loud music, strange tastes, and disgusting sights.

Those dreams get caught in that dream catcher. But then there's a problem. They try to escape. They're wrecking that dream catcher. *The notes are flopping around discordantly. They won't give up, and they start to go crazy as they try to break free. In an effort to preserve the dream catcher, a.k.a. save myself, I begin to shut down.* The things that bother me—those are the things that basically wreck the dream catcher. *Those are the things that tangle up my brain.*

The problem is that I try my best to cut out noise, and, sometimes, when I'm not paying attention, there are some noises I don't hear. It could be psychological, but I can't really say it's not just physical, either.

What are some of the things you see that bother you?

I can't stand looking at some of the food my dad eats. I can't look at a lot of foods, like soups that have mixed up meats and mashed up vegetables in them. I don't know what some of the foods he eats are called, but when I see that food, even if I don't smell it, I always feel sick to my stomach. It looks so unpleasant to eat; I don't want to look at it.

Another thing I can't stand to look at is feces. The thing is, I can handle looking at gore. I can handle most things I see, but I can't handle feces. Those are things I don't feel comfortable seeing. They make me feel uneasy.

I also hate looking at something dirty—for example, a table at a restaurant that was just used. When I look at it, if there were people sitting at that table and they have just left, I have wait until it is cleared. One thing is for sure—I am not a germophobe. I don't have a problem eating anything that has just dropped on the ground. I don't really care about the 5-second-rule thing—it's actually complete nonsense.

Part of it is that, at some moments, I'm a little uncomfortable about touching certain things. I'm worried that they might be sticky. When I eat something off the floor, it's something I've accidentally dropped. I know what it is, and I walked on the floor, so I know it's dry. When some things are wet, or I can actually see a stain, I do get worried, because I don't know if it's something sticky or slimy, which I know I can't handle feeling. If I accidentally rest my arm on that area, I might regret that feeling. At restaurants, I will react to the soap or whatever the person was using to wash the table. It depends on how it feels when you have a cleaning fluid on this kind of table. When I'm looking at debris on the table, I don't know if it's water, and I don't want to risk it. I don't want it to be anything sticky. My senses can overreact to it, just like when I touch paint, and I don't like the feeling—it's irritating.

Do you have any pets? Are you a pet person?

No. I am not a pet person at all. At times I feel like I can have a pet around, and at other times, I don't feel I can. I just can't really handle having a pet. *I have so much trouble trying to take care of myself,* I don't think I would be able to take care of an animal.

Plus, I'm a person who likes to keep things pretty clean, and I would be constantly worried that the animal would leave something or do something that makes me feel uneasy. Others might say, "Oh yeah, well you'll get used to it." But, it doesn't change the fact that I have an uncomfortable feeling toward animals.

It's like a phobia, akin to being scared of the dark. If you sat in the dark, in a corner, someone might say, "Nothing's going to happen to you in the dark." But you still feel concerned when you think of being in the dark, all alone. It's the same thing with me and animals. While it's not a phobia, I do feel uneasy around them. Also, animals tend to make some noises that bother me. Parrots constantly make that loud chirping noise.

Another problem I have—and this is something that happens with people with my disorder—is that I can't deal with a lot of people talking about different and random topics at the same time or people talking on their cell phones. I have a big

issue when people around me are talking on their cell phones.
You know how I said that when I'm in a noisy place, my mind
is going around in different places, questioning what each of
them is saying? My mind goes bonkers. When I'm hearing
these conversations, and I'm hearing all these random voices,
and each one muffles out the other, I can't distinguish each
person's voice as separate from another. One woman says,
"Hey, how are you doing?" while another person says, "I have
a severe headache," while another person says, "Where's the
mustard?" Everything blends into a mess of words. You hear
"Blah, blah, blah," and it's just a bunch of noise, which annoys
me. When there's a private conversation going on, and I can
make out what they're saying, it can make things even worse
for me. When it comes to my dad and his business, he talks on
his cell phone a lot, and I tell him to stop doing it. If my dad
talks on his cell phone for more than 10 minutes, maybe even
15 minutes to a half hour, or even an hour, my mind starts
going crazy.

I don't know how to explain it. It's actually a different
reaction than with other situations. When my dad talked for
over a half an hour once on his cell phone, my body was moving around. I couldn't stay still. My eyes were wider, and I
felt so irritated that I wanted to bang my head on something.
I kept pulling at my hair, my teeth were clenched tight, and
I was making weird noises. Every time I looked at my dad,
I thought, "Just get off the phone!" I felt like I was going to
burst into tears. I just kept on moving around, and I didn't
want to start rolling on the ground, because when my mind
goes off like that, I don't know whether I should say something
or not. I don't know if my dad will get mad at me or not. If I
can't get an answer about what I should do in my head, it's

kind of a crazy feeling. I'm going crazy with different thoughts in my head. Should I say yes, should I say no? Maybe it's okay to say something. What if my dad yells at me if I do this? It's like that. It's always like that. I react this way because I'm hearing this whole subject, and this is a subject I am so un-aware of that my mind is wondering, what is my dad saying? What is this? And because I don't understand the conversation, and I don't know exactly what they're talking about, it just builds up and goes wrong in my head. It really irritates me to the point where I go almost insane. And I think it's because it's a long conversation, and I'm trying to think of what they said before. I forget what he said earlier. My mind gets over-whelmed to the point where it really wants to shut off, and yet I'm still overthinking. It's like a computer running very slowly on its battery. The computer wants to turn off all its programs to save energy, but it keeps running, just very slowly. That's what's happening to me. My mind refuses to shut off.

When I explain this to my dad, he tries not to talk too long on the phone, and this really makes me happy. I think one of the reasons I never mentioned it to my dad before was because those phone conversations were usually rare. They didn't hap-pen too often. But, they do happen. And I do get those feelings when they do. Some days, when other people talk on their cell phones, I get a little irritated and annoyed. But some days, when the conversations get longer, my annoyance can get worse. People talking on their cell phones is one of the biggest problems I have.

Even during a basic conversation, I tend to get that same feeling—not to that extreme, but I do. Like when I'm in a loud, noisy restaurant. I can't cover my ears, so I get a head-ache. Many conversations going on at once frustrate me. But it is worse with cell phones, because when it comes to cell phones, you don't hear what's happening on the other line. You just hear one person talking. That tends to bother me more, because now my mind's going, "Is he talking to a man? A woman? Who is he talking to? Is this really important? Is the guy even listening to him?" I think because my mind is questioning things over and over again, I just want my dad to get to the point on the phone, and end the call. If he keeps talking longer, I'm going to keep questioning myself about the conversation and why it's taking so long. And that's when my mind goes into its crazy spin. "Is the subject that big of a deal? Is the subject really important? Is the subject really necessary? Does that subject have to do with global warming? Is that subject going to help world peace? Is that subject really going to make my life better? Is that subject really going to kill me in the next 2 minutes?" When I'm hearing something about a subject or a conversation that I don't know about, I'm always irritated or let down. And I guess that's also why I had trouble being in school.

I thought many of the things I was taught in school were pointless. For instance, I thought they put too much pressure on us by making us do math problems that we're not even going to use in real life. It's the same problem. When we're talking about a subject that I don't understand or see, I feel like there is no reason for it to be this complicated. My mind just keeps asking questions, and it snowballs.

Alex, one of your images is a dream catcher. Would you give us a little history on that, please?

Well, it's not one of my favorite images. But I do know what it represents, which helped me think of a way to explain some of my Asperger's traits. When I was a kid I used to have nightmares, and I had problems going to sleep. My mom came up with something that would protect me from having nightmares. She had me close my eyes, and she kissed both my eyes and my forehead. She created a "triangle barrier" of love. And, she told me that it would get rid of the bad things.

A few weeks or months later, she got me a dream catcher. It was a very simple one. She probably bought it at a five-dollar store. It was a basic, blue ring, with simple netting. It had two long strings, with colored beads and feathers. I hung it up on the wall next to my bed, and I've always kept it up there, no matter what. I know one day, I'll have to throw it out. Actually, you know what? Nowadays, I don't feel like I dream at all. I have a few dreams here and there, and I remember a few of them. But, I don't think I dream a lot these days.

Do you think the dream catcher helped you? Or do you think having your mother kiss your eyes helped?

In all honesty, I know these remedies were psychological in nature. I know that the dream catcher and my mom's kisses put that psychology in my head that said, "I'm not going to have a nightmare tonight." So, I know that was the case.

What Relaxes Me

Cartoons, video games, movies, drinks, and food

What are some of things that relax you?

Listening to music, watching something on my computer, and drinking my favorite soda. I also do physical things to help me relax. Sometimes I pace. I even tend to flinch a lot; my hands start flinching. I tend to move back and forth in my seat. I twitch my head a bit, and I breathe more heavily. Part of that is to avoid having a panic attack. Also, I try occupy my mind when I'm in the middle of having a panic attack or I find myself in the middle of an environment where I'm not comfortable. Basically, the reason why I do repetitive things is:

1. To keep myself comfortable with being in a strange reality or different environment.
2. So I don't end up panicking or completely shutting down. I don't know what might really happen to me if I didn't have these rituals to prevent me from panicking.

Society may say that people with Asperger's should be taught to give up their idiosyncrasies that are not "normal." What are your thoughts on this?

Simply put, if these little quirks are not destructive and are not hurting myself or other people, it is more important that I, or other people with Asperger's, be relaxed, rather than try to please the standards of society.

What about watching cartoons as a form of relaxation?

I enjoy cartoons; they help me to relax. For example, I like SpongeBob, and I enjoy some old familiar favorites, like Rocco's Modern Life, which was a fun cartoon I loved when I was a kid. I still like it today.

The main reason I love watching cartoons is because I'm looking at a totally different world. And I think another reason is that it's a world created by other people's minds. In that world, it's their rules, and their setting, even though the cartoons may flow the same way as real life dramas do. In some ways, I think I enjoy cartoons because that they are all drawn, or they are all computer animated. The authors take advantage of the medium by giving it its own laws. Things like the laws of gravity or the laws of actual physics don't always apply in those cartoons, and it allows the cartoonists to do whatever they want.

For me, this makes it so much more enjoyable to watch. Things happen that you'd never see in real life. It's like eye candy, but it can also be combined with well-thought-out stories. And, considering how expensive it is to make live-action stretch the standards of disbelief, cartoons are another way to create fantasized worlds without a large expense.

What do you think of people who question if adults should watch cartoons?

When I made the video "In My Mind," there were a lot of people who said, "You're never too old for cartoons. I'm an adult, and I watch them, too!"

But then I ask, "How many times do you actually watch cartoons? How many times do you watch the cartoons by yourself? Do you actually watch them intentionally? Are they first on your list?" For me, out of all the options I have available, I like cartoons the best. They relax me the most.

People with Asperger's have other ways to relax. What are yours?

I drink Dr Pepper to relieve my nerves. I also like Diet Pepsi, but I prefer Dr Pepper.

Why Dr Pepper? It has a unique taste to it that feels very sweet, warm, and soothing to me. When I drink it, it relaxes me as it goes down my throat. So when I feel stressed or upset, I drink a Dr Pepper to help ease the pain away. It distracts me, which relaxes me.

It's like when little kids have ice cream. They like having a dessert; it makes them happy. It's the same way I feel when I drink a Dr Pepper. It drowns some of my sorrows away and has a nice feel to it. Although it's not that good for you, it's not the worst drink, either.

There are a lot of drinks I don't like, and one of those is water. I'm not quite sure how to explain it, but it might be the way water feels in my throat that I don't like. My body has a hard time trying to swallow it. To me, it doesn't really work out. I have tried using mixes that give water some flavor, but all of it still has the similar aftertaste that I don't like, and I haven't found a flavor that I like, either. I tried drinking diet green tea, which I found okay, but I thought if I drank too much of it, I'd get sick of it—which I did.

What kinds of food do you like?

I should mention here that I don't have a great diet. I don't tend to remember all the foods I eat, but there's really not a lot of variety. I eat the same thing 3 days straight, or even 4 days in a row. I eat pizza, fries, and pasta with Parmesan cheese—no sauce, no butter—just Parmesan. It has a comforting taste to it that relieves my stress, as well.

What was your favorite food when you were a kid?

I'm not really sure what my favorite foods were when I was a kid, but one of my longtime favorites is pasta or spaghetti. And I don't mean spaghetti with meat sauce, as most people probably like. What I have is plain spaghetti with Parmesan cheese. I douse it in Parmesan cheese. I love the flavor of spaghetti. I consider it to be like Dr Pepper—it is a comforting food, it has a nice warm feel, the flavor is simple, and it tastes delicious. The Parmesan rolls around in my mouth, while the spaghetti adds a little bit of flavor when it goes down my throat. It's another relaxing taste for me.

Besides pasta, I also like very simple, plain pizza or pizza with pepperoni. Plain chicken fingers and French fries are my favorites, too. It's actually really hard for me to remember most of the foods I like, and I know that's hard to believe, because there aren't many foods I like! There are only a few of them. But still, when I try to say what my favorite foods are, I have trouble identifying them. I like other things besides pizza, such as McDonald's and Burger King, where I get just a plain hamburger with ketchup, buns, and meat. I also eat plain hot dogs with buns—no relish, no ketchup, and no mustard. But, I can't remember most other foods, and I can't quite depict my favorites—I just remember pasta and spaghetti.

We just reviewed the foods you like. It seems to me they're heavily saturated with cholesterol. What if your doctor said, "Alex, you have to give up those foods!"

I can't. They're the only things I like. I can't force myself to eat any other things, because my body won't let me eat them. Not all of them are saturated in fats, you know. The hot dog is 100 percent pure meat. McDonald's—I know, that's the real garbage. I can't stop eating those basic foods. They're the only things that I can eat. But I'm not particularly worried too much, because I don't eat too much of them. I try to keep a nice level of how much I eat—the proper serving size, if you will.

Some youngsters with Asperger's get very excited or overwhelmed; they'll pat their heads or clap their hands. What are some of the physical reactions you have when you get overloaded?

It's the same thing for me, when it comes to having breaking down. My mind goes crazy, I start to shake with excitement, I move around sometimes, my mind can't think straight, and I try my best to do the usual stuff I can do to calm down. Sometimes my body will flinch, it will jitter, and I try my best to calm it down by having the usual Dr Pepper. But, it can be hard to handle when I get really surprised or overwhelmed by a situation.

Why do I sway back and forth when I stand? I don't know how to explain it. It's one of the most common things that happens with the disorder. I just can't stand still. That's the basic point. When I'm lying in bed, when I'm sitting down, when I'm resting, of course I don't move. But when you're standing, you're using some of your energy to stand on your own two feet. And I can't stand still when I'm using some of that energy. I don't know how anyone else is able to stand perfectly still! I really don't know how they do it. All I know is that when I stand, there are a lot of different things that go on. One, there's pressure being put on my legs, and my feet get tired, so I sway back and forth to let them get a slight moment to breathe. There are some moments my legs would start jittering if I stood too still, so swaying helps get them in motion a bit. It's the thing I need to do to keep myself comfortable while standing. And, unfortunately, if you're expecting me to stand still for a family photo, you're not going to get it.

My Schooling

Adapting to school life

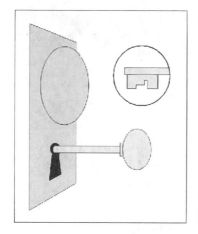 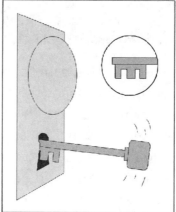

When you first began school, what were some of your first difficulties?

I would get headaches from loud noises, and some people thought that when I said to them, "Please stop making that loud noise—please stop singing," I was just being difficult. But the truth is, I wasn't. In school, some of the kids wondered why I listened to music when I asked them to be quiet with their own music. Well, my mind is like door. The thing I listen to or feel, taste, or touch, is like a key. And some keys can fit into the keyhole and turn, which make me feel relaxed and calm. But there are some keys that do not have the right kind of teeth. They get pushed in and jerked around, causing me irritation and all sorts of head pain.

IN MY MIND

Describe the noises in the school that bothered you. What were they like?

It was the noise that some of my classmates made. I didn't have it at home. Some just couldn't stay quiet—they couldn't really stay quiet. In fact, the teachers would yell and tell them to keep quiet, but in the end they always kept talking and wouldn't lower their voices. When I heard the racket they made when they were yelling at each other, it was a scramble of different words that did not flow together into my brain.

If the crowd of all the students involved each of them talking about different subjects with different people and they were talking quietly, it might be less aggravating. But if they were loud, it would become a torment. Every time I went to school and it became louder, I would try to yell out, "Quiet!" But even then, they often didn't listen. In fact, sometimes I would get in trouble because I wanted quiet, and they just wouldn't do it.

Some of my teachers understood me, and some let me leave the room. When I had teachers who didn't, I was stuck in the room. It seemed that the only times I was able to leave the classroom were when I was in tears or really didn't feel well.

How often would you cry, and have you outgrown it?

Back then, it happened a lot. As for outgrowing it, I would say in some ways I have, but in other ways, I haven't. It's not always easy to say. I haven't kept track of how many times I've cried or how many times I've cried in previous years.

Tell us your difficulties in school regarding how you sit and what the school did to accommodate you.

One of the things that bothered me the most in school was that some classmates would ask, "Alex, why don't you sit normally, like everyone else? Why do you have to have your legs up?" I always tried to explain it to them, but they asked, "Have you ever tried putting your legs down? Have you ever really tried?" They kept on asking me about it. I would sometimes get the same question from the same classmate later in the year. Most of them just didn't get it. I can't sit normally. It's just how I am.

This was before I knew I had a disorder. And my classmates didn't know I had a disorder, either. So of course they were not fully informed when it came to understanding why I was different from everyone else.

One of the worst things about school was my music class. For months, I had to sit in a normal position. It took a while before my father was able to get me out of that situation. The teacher was demanding and insensitive. He used to yell at students, as well, which was also irritating for me. He would yell at kids whenever they made the smallest mistake. (I'm sorry, mister, but this is music class—not boot camp!)

Whenever I sat Indian style and he spotted me, he always made me to put my legs down. Every single time that happened, I was so uncomfortable. I lost concentration. It was a really long hour in that class. I couldn't wait for the clock to strike. It seemed like the days got longer and longer. So when people now ask me, "Have you tried putting your legs down?" I can say, "Yes, I was forced to do it in school. And it hurt. And no matter how many times I did it, it never got better, and I never got used to it. My dream came true when my father told me I no longer had to take that class. It was a godsend.

Besides that, there were other things that went on in school that were a problem. One of the biggest issues was that many of the desk chairs were too small for me. Because I sat Indian style, the regular desk chairs tended to make my legs slip out, and I usually had to hold on to the desk.

Another issue was that the desks were literally welded together. So I couldn't move them. They were so cramped, and the metal bar was in the way when I sat with my knees Indian style. I told the school officials about this, and they tried to fix it. They did attempt to get a special desk, which was a desk made for kids who are overweight.

Kids who are overweight have special chairs designed to be a little bit larger, so they can sit better. When the desks arrived, I was happy, but, unfortunately, there was another issue. The chair was wider, but it wasn't longer, so the desk wasn't really big enough.

I remember I had a problem in wood shop—there were always stools, and I can't handle stools. They're too small. But there was this one revolving stool, which was designed as a chair, and I have to say, it was fun! That was the chair I always liked to take because it's much larger, and I was able to sit Indian style quite comfortably.

I do remember the first day the teacher said to me, "You know, you're the first student I've seen who sits Indian style on a stool." However, there were other students who wanted that stool chair besides me. Some of them tried to claim it. And I didn't know what to say to convince them that I needed that chair. I guess this is what led up to my creative solution.

When someone else took that chair, I took two stools and put them together, so I could put my legs together.

When I did this, I realized it was the solution to my desk problem. So, when I went to class, I took two chairs and placed them together. I continued to do this throughout the rest of the school year. And I have to say, it really was helpful. Ever since then, almost any restaurant or place I go to, if they have very small chairs or no big benches, or couches, I will take two of those chairs and place them together so I can sit Indian style. Sometimes when I go to a restaurant and have my chairs set up like that, I still get people who stare at me because not only am I sitting with my legs up, but I have the chairs positioned differently.

When you were younger, what was your relationship with kids in your class?

It's not really something I'm always happy to talk about. There were times I felt like I had friends, but in the end, I never did. And I would say that today, that still applies. When I was in school, when I was young, I behaved so differently than others. No one knew I had a disorder, and they just didn't associate with me. When you're 5 to 8 years old, maybe 10 or 12, you're still not really aware of the disorder.

Of course, your classmates aren't really told a lot about it, either. I might have been more of an outcast when I was younger than when I was older, because when I was young, the other students didn't know anything about my issues. And, to be honest, I almost had moments where I felt like my classmates didn't like me, or that they didn't understand me, or that they thought that I was an odd freak.

There was one day in gym, where all the classmates were together, and they had to do what the gym coach said. And this was a test class, where you had to test each other. There were physical tests. So you had to do things like pushups and pull-ups, however many you could do in this time limit. And then you were graded on what you could do. One of the coaches had a timed test, where he gave you two blocks, and you had to run back and forth, depositing the blocks. The fastest time you got was part of your grade. Everyone gathered around to take turns, and whenever someone took off, the others cheered. They shouted, "Woo!" "Yeah!" "Go! Go! Go!" It was fun to see them all do that. They did it for every single classmate. And then it was my turn.

And when I took my turn, it was just silent. No one cheered for me. No one said anything. They just watched. Out of about 20 kids, I was the only one nobody cheered for. I don't know if they did it because I don't like loud noises—but I doubt that was the reason. They just didn't understand me, or they didn't like me back then. But, it's something that still goes through my mind a lot. I know that if you were a bad kid, or if you were a jerk to everyone, it is understandable why they would not cheer a person on. I can understand that you would not be respected by your classmates for being that way. I know that if you were cheered by a lot of people, you could get a few boos from the bullies. But, the fact that the whole class didn't say anything, just nothing at all, and I hadn't even done anything to them, made me sad. I was a person who stayed mostly in the corner, trying to do classwork like everyone else. It is heartbreaking every time I think of it. It was one of the first signs that other kids didn't like me or weren't interested in me.

There were other things in class that went the same way. When I was at lunch and was eating my food, I remember there were always people who asked me why I always sat the way I did or why did I have this problem, or why did I do this or that. I remember I overheard this going on once, and I bet they knew I could hear them—this was another hurtful thing. Everyone sat at a distance from me at lunchtime. You may have seen it in shows, where a kid does something mean to his classmates—he may have treated them badly or done something to ruin their fun. So, when he wants to sit at the table with them, they just abandon the table.

Of course, I've never really experienced that, but barely anyone sat with me. I sat in one area, and there was distance between me and the other kids. One time I was sitting in the corner, and someone was about to sit down, and they mentioned that they were uncomfortable being near me. One person replied with, "What's the big deal? He doesn't do anything. All he does is eat. So just sit over there, it's not a problem." I have to say, I felt happy to hear someone say they felt like it wasn't a big deal. But, the fact that people had a problem sitting next to me was just another thing that went through my mind at that stage of my life.

When it came to my late primary school years or middle school, I knew about my disorder, and everybody else started to know, too. I felt like more and more of an outcast. It's always really hurtful for me to recall a lot of this sad truth. I guess I can't always blame them. They were kids, just like me, and they were not aware of my disorder.

Throughout your school days, were you ever bullied or teased by your classmates?

No, not really. I would say this—I think I was lucky. Even though I felt like an outcast, I was in a small school. And in a small school, everybody knows everybody else. So if a child does something wrong, parents are informed, and that parent will tell another parent, and they'll go right to the person who started it. I don't recall any moments of bullying happening much at school. I don't think I was ever teased or bullied at all. No one ever forced me to give him my lunch money; no one beat me down verbally. And, no one tried to insult me.

I know there may not have been bullies, but there were people with bad attitudes. They were ruder to me than others. The only downside to being in a small school is that you're even more of an outcast, when it comes down to it. When you go to a school with over a thousand people, your chances of being bullied increase. I remember being told that one high school had over a thousand students in one graduating class. And I could tell you one thing—you could be an outcast there, but at least you're going to be able to find someone who has the same thing you have!

Going to a small school had one advantage. There weren't many bullies. I don't know what the odds of bullying are, but I'm pretty sure the odds at a small school are fairly low. You might come across jerks in school, of course. But when it comes to bullies who are big and tough and take your money, it doesn't happen here. Everybody knows everyone here, so it's not easy to hide your identity when you're a bully. But, that said, even though I think I was lucky, I feel like I was probably more of an outsider because I attended a small school. If you go to a school with 5,000 students, and the average number of people who are born with autism or Asperger's syndrome is probably one in 200, then there are some odds that you will find about 40 people who have the same disorder as you in that entire school. You should be able to find a couple of friends who can relate to you perfectly. For me, I was in a school with 200 students altogether. Can you guess how many people had a diagnosis of Asperger's syndrome or autism during my time in school? Just one person. Me.

It was only when I was nearing the end of high school that there was a new kindergartner or middle-schooler with autism or Asperger's. So, I was really the only one in my school on the spectrum, and I didn't have many friends.

The kids at Shelter Island didn't tease you. Do you think that was out of respect? Did you always walk at the end of the line, and why?

No, I don't think it was out of respect. In fact, I can definitely tell it was not out of respect because I was a tattletale. That is still true when it comes to my family—especially my sister and younger brother. No matter that I'm 21 or so; I call my dad when they do something wrong.

In school, if someone did something to me, I told on them. I was not going to hide it—I was going to tell. Even if they said, "I'll hurt you if you tell!" I still told on them. And even if people called me a tattletale, I didn't mind. Some kids consider being a tattletale a bad thing, but if someone insulted me or did something mean, I always told my teacher. I was stayed close to my teachers in school. So if someone did something wrong, I instantly reported it. I was very sensitive. So that may have been a reason why they never tried to bully me, because I always ended up telling on them. I guess you could say I was a type of teacher's pet. Not in the sense of intelligence, or always raising my hand, or always helping a teacher out, but in the sense of always telling the teacher when something happened.

The answer about being in the back of the line is, no, I wasn't. To be honest, I was always one of those kids who wanted to be in the front of the line. I think it was for a few reasons. One, when you're in the front, you get things over with first. I don't really want to stand around, waiting for things to happen. I want to sit back and get my mind back to thinking about other things. And when you go to lunch, you always want to be first in line for lunch, because you want to get your food first, and then you have more time to eat it. Also, if you're in the front, you don't have to see everyone's face or reactions when they're behind you.

I would say I felt comfortable being in the front of the line, but not the back. When it comes to being in the car, I always prefer to be in the front seat, rather than the back seat. In the past, my family members used to get annoyed with me, because my sister and brother were always arguing about why I got to sit up front. Or, they would say it was their turn to sit in front. Nowadays, it seems everybody knows that Alex gets the front all the time. It's just because of my comfort level. I need to be comfortable; there is more room up front for me to sit Indian style. And when you're in front, there's no one in front of your face, covering up what's ahead of you. I know where I am and where I'm going. In the back, I have someone sitting in front of me, and I can't always tell what's out there.

It's the same thing when it comes to standing in line.

What is your reaction when you sense that you're being ridiculed?

Even though no one really picked on me in school, there was one time I would say I was insulted. I said something in class, and another kid said sarcastically, "Stop doing that—you're hurting my ears!" And he put his hands over his ears. When that happened, I felt very angry and upset, because he was mocking me.

But, in all honesty, after making my video, I would say I'm a stronger man, who doesn't let other people get to me when they ridicule me.

13

My Family

My parents, sisters, and brother

Alex, tell us about your family life.

Even though my mind works differently, and even though I require a lot of things, it doesn't really change my family's life. It doesn't make my family any different from any other family. My family has to make different choices to help me handle this world. But, it doesn't mean their whole lives are changed. It doesn't mean I'm a vegetable, and they're spending their whole lives taking care of me. I can still move, and I can walk and talk and do some chores here and there.

But, you know, there are still some differences with me. My disorder does require my family to make slight changes to make things work out for me. For example, I feel awkward, and my sister feels awkward sometimes, when she has to drive me places. This is my younger sister by 3 years or so, and she has to be the one to drive me around. I cannot drive, and it sometimes makes me uncomfortable when she has to pick me up and she has friends in the car. Imagine what she might be feeling when her friends are in the car and they're asking, "Katie, why doesn't your older brother just drive his own car?" And I think she has to respond that I can't drive.

My family has to put up with the fact that we have to make two meals at dinnertime. Since I'm a picky eater and someone who doesn't like certain foods, imagine when my father has to make chicken pot pie, and, on the side, he has to cook some pasta for me. He has to cook two dishes, even though everyone else eats chicken pot pie. I know most other families have dinner and they cook one thing, but I'm different, so I stick out.

One of my difficulties at dinnertime is that there are many conversations going on at once. It may be one of the reasons why I hate eating dinner at the table with my family. I've never liked eating at the table. And I think the reason for this is that they're talking about topics where I have no clue about what they're saying. And my mind is boggling like crazy, and I just want to eat. When it comes to my brother or my sister talking about their problems at school, I'm thinking, "What is the problem? I don't know." And it ends up bothering my mind.

Another thing that probably annoys my family happens during dinnertime. Some foods I do like, and some of them have to be cooked just right. It doesn't annoy my father, but sometimes I feel guilty about it. I do this, and my sister rolls her eyes at me.

There are times when my dad makes chicken wings or legs, and he makes them with pepper and salt. I like that in some ways, but sometimes there's a problem with that, and they have to be well cooked. They can't be red, they can't be juicy, and they have to be well done. They have to have the right amount of salt and pepper. So when it comes to the point where I eat the meat, and I feel that it doesn't taste right, and I see a lot of redness in it, I say to my dad, "I don't think I can eat these chicken legs." It's up to my dad to get it off of the table and begin cooking a different meal. It's not that much of a big deal for him, because he knows my choices for food are essentially the same three or four dishes: pasta, nachos, pizza—mostly easy-to-prepare food. It doesn't make it hard for him. But, this is something my family has sacrificed for me.

My family members also do more chores than I do. I only do one chore a day, and it's one chore I really hate. I don't even understand why; it's just unloading the dishwasher. I think it's tedious, and doing it for my whole life has made me sick of it.

My family tends to go on vacations without me. And no, it's not because they want to get away from me. They want to go on a vacation, but unfortunately, I'm the anchor that says, "I don't like to go on vacation, and I don't want to go on vacation." Usually they stay with me, but sometimes they head off on their own. And I don't have too much of a problem with that.

Now tell us about growing up with your brother and sisters and your mom and dad. Would you reflect on all of these people in your life? How they might have helped you, or what you found difficult.

My mom and dad are great in some ways. I'll talk about my brother and sisters first.

I have two sisters and one brother. One sister is older than me, and one sister is younger, and my brother is much younger. My older sister's name is Brittany, my younger sister is named Katie, and my brother is named Chandler. When it comes to my older sister Brittany, I think we get along just fine. She is always nice, she is always kind, I always enjoy being around her, and she enjoys being around me. She was actually the "good sister"—the nice, sweet one. On the other hand, I never seemed to get along with my younger sister and brother as well. But that was mostly because, well, that's what brothers and sisters do. They fight with each other. They get into trouble for fighting about things. Some things are not even that important. But, it's just a common thing.

Part of it was that they didn't understand me back then. I didn't understand myself much, either. I didn't understand people, and I didn't understand what they thought. I didn't know how people behaved so differently, compared to me. To me, when I'm looking at everyone else, everyone seems to be odd. Say that I'm an American in Japan. I'm looking around, and I see different things, different people, and a different culture that I don't understand. Of course, everyone in Japan will be looking at me, because I'm behaving so differently from them. I'm waving rather than bowing, I'm eating with a fork instead of chopsticks. When they're looking at me, they think I'm like an alien from another planet. But, to be honest, I'm feeling like an astronaut on another planet, and they are the aliens. So you could say that is what it felt like when I was a kid.

I don't know what to say about how I coped with it in the past. Brothers and sisters argue with each other. A family in which one brother is autistic and the other isn't is not going to be that different. Sure, one might get the upper hand because he has a disorder, and a parent can defend him. But one of the biggest difficulties that parents have to worry about is they don't know the proper time to tell their child that he has a disorder or his siblings that their brother has a disorder. If the siblings do not know this is the problem, it seems like the parents are just defending the kid who is autistic. If they don't tell the kid or his brother and sisters that he's autistic, or that his mind works differently than others, then it ends up feeling like he's the favorite. It can lead to more arguments and more problems. Especially because they might result from differences in his behavior. My brother and sisters could not quite understand why I got to do things that they were forbidden to do. It's one of the big problems that families have to learn to deal with. They need to build an equal set of feelings toward each other. The best thing is to try to help each kid understand the others.

My parents are good to me, in most cases. Since I don't understand sometimes, I never really felt like I could understand what they do. In the past, one of my biggest problems was that my mother used to yell a lot. But, it wasn't her fault. She was yelling at us because it's what a lot of parents do. When kids get into trouble, when kids do something bad, parents yell. They tell the kids that they're doing something wrong. The problem with me is that I have problems with loud noises. But, my parents didn't know I had this disorder. But when she was treating me like everyone else, which was a good thing in most ways, it still could lead up to worse problems for me. One thing is that when it comes to people with a disorder, you want to treat them like everyone else. On the other hand, you want to treat them in a way that will help them feel like they fit in, and you don't want to wreck their comfort zone. For example, if you have me over for dinner, you're going to let me sit differently (Indian style); you're going to let me talk. You're going to be sure to lower your voice a bit; you're not going to yell out loud. You're going to try to help me feel like I fit in and feel like everyone else. That's what my mom and dad did with me.

As I grew up, Dad and Mom didn't really yell anymore. My brother and sisters are more understanding, and we don't tend to fight anymore.

My dad always has to be prepared for a problem. My inability to drive is one of the big issues. My dad does take me out of the house; he has to drive me around. He leaves work to help me get around. I would say the other sacrifice he makes is that he spends a lot of money on me. Sometimes when I'm feeling like I've had a rough week, he'll lend me a few dollars to buy a video game to mess around with, in hopes that it will occupy me for few days. Even though there are a lot of things my family does for me, it's not really much different than what other families do for each other. I'm sure my family is different from yours, but, in reality, most families have oddities that make us all alike in one way or another.

Would you tell us how your father has helped you over the years, and what kind of father is he?

My dad really is one of the people has who made me who I am. He's extremely caring. He tries his best. I would give him the World's Best Dad Award, but I can't, because he gets so caught up in his work, and he tends to get tired often. He's not perfect, but he's like every other good dad. He tries his best, but he's not that perfect, idealistic, smiling father, who can make his kids rich and very successful in college and make them feel happy and give them every bit of advice that instantly solves all of their problems. There's no such thing as the perfect father. But, I have to say, he comes close. He comes very close, not because he tries to give advice, which sometimes he does.

Let me tell you, if the world's greatest father was a person who gives out lame jokes, he will win. I must tell you that every joke he says is appallingly awful. Any bad comedian would be crying tears of joy, knowing that at least their acts are not as horrible as my father's act. And yet, he still tries and tries and tries. He still does things that annoy me, even though he doesn't mean to. Parents embarrass their kids.

Sometimes I get a little embarrassed. And with some of the things he does, he doesn't mean to be annoying. However, saying something in a weird way, or singing something out makes me a little embarrassed.

My father really does try his best. He does everything he can to help me out. He tries to take me places where I really need to go. He helps me out with all my problems. He tries his best on everything. He always went to my school to talk with my teachers to help me find solutions for my problems. He does tend to work a lot, which is irritating to me. But, I know that part of it is because he has to run a business. I wish I had him to myself more often.

At home, if my sister starts to argue with me because she thinks that I'm doing something all wrong, like putting too much sugar in my cereal, she will say, "That's too much sugar." My dad will say, "Stop bothering him. Let him do what he wants to do." I'm always surprised by how well my dad is able to understand me. He doesn't understand everything perfectly, but he does understand me.

I know people who read this book are maybe looking for some advice from me. I'm not a parent, and I know I'm never going to be a parent for multiple reasons. But, my father has to put up with me every day, and he seems to know what he's doing. He doesn't know everything he needs to do for me, but he seems to know the most.

How much do you depend on your dad, and why?

Right now, I depend on him a lot, for a lot of reasons. I am not fully prepared to live on my own yet—I'm working on it, but

I'm not fully ready. To be honest, my dad knows what to do, and he always seems to know how to help me. He's the only person I can really get some help from. Something happens, and I get nervous, and the first thing I think of is to call my dad—no one else.

If I know my dad is off-island, I can't really make a decision on whom to call. I always have to call him first to ask him whom I can ask to solve a problem I might have. I depend on him a lot because I'm not in that kind of position yet to handle my own decisions. Once I find my confidence, which I am working on, I will be able to handle it. But as of now, I'm stuck with really needing my father for almost everything.

> Would you say that you depend on your father all the time, or do you try to be as independent as you can?

It varies. There are times I know that I have a choice. But there are other times where I just don't know how to handle it, so I instantly think to call my dad. My mind goes crazy unless I first ask him. But he may not be around, or he may not pick up his phone, so in the moment of panic, I end up having to going with my decision. I sometimes regret it, because I feel like I've made the wrong decision. It's crazy, the things that go through my mind.

I try my best to be independent, and a lot of times I am. There are certainly moments where I have to make a big choice, even though to most people, it might seem like no problem. Sometimes I can't stop my mind, and it starts doing one thing: It overthinks every single question. So, I can't think of the right answer to go with.

Have you tried to get other people to advise you on how to make decisions?

I think I have tried, and at times it works, but I'm just so used to my father that I keep going back to him. I have tried asking others for help, but it's not something that I'm that used to. So you could say it's a force of habit.

Do you see your dependency on your dad as part of not growing up?

I don't want to get rid of my child. Some people feel that when you grow up, you want to push that inner child away. But, I don't want to get rid of what makes me a child. I don't want to get rid of my youth. I don't want to get rid of the things that make me enjoy the things I like, no matter how old I am. And, I understand the idea of pushing a child to grow up to help him be more independent, but with most people, something always occurs to set off a chain reaction. And I don't want to risk pushing the child part away for independence, because it might push other parts of my child away.

If you got the news tomorrow that your dad was in the hospital with a very serious illness, what would your reaction be? And what are the thoughts that would go through your head? And how would you deal with that?

I'm really not sure. I would need help. Until I could find someone else to be by my side for a long time, that could help me
out and be a helping hand for the rest of my life—the only
person I have now is my dad, sometimes my mom, Liza, sometimes Kate, and my grandparents. Of course, I would be more
worried about him, because if he really were not doing well, I
wouldn't know what to think about how I would survive. If he
is ill, I am ill.

Not in the sense that I feel sick, but in the sense that for
me, for a handicapped person, he or she needs a wheelchair to
get around. My dad is part of my wheelchair, to get me around
at the moment. I will always need people to help me, especially
when my parents are not around later in my life. But right
now, I don't have that replacement yet. If I lose that part of
the wheelchair, I'm immobile. I can't do anything. If I couldn't
call my dad if I had a problem, then I wouldn't know what to
do. Most likely, I would be in the corner, with my mind racing on many different fronts, about my father and myself, just
trying to figure out how I would be able to handle each day. I
might come up with some solutions here and there, but I am
so unaware of things, I really don't know how to figure things
out when something happens. When I shut down, and someone
asks me a question, I say, "I don't know," and I can't think of
an answer. If I don't have a solution, I can just call dad. He
knows me the best; he has taken care of me the longest; he
knows how to handle things the best. So I know he can give
me an answer that I can't come up with myself. But if I know
I can't do that, something builds up in me. If something were
to happen to my father, it would be like my own world crum-
bling down, and I feel like I'd be completely. I just hope I find
the solution to my problems before anything like that happens,

because if I don't have the people that are helping me to get around places, helping me cope with the world—I don't know what will happen when the person who solves my problems goes away.

You just told me that your brother went into the hospital. I'd like to know your emotional response. How you feel about that inside?

It was a surprise when I heard Dad mention that Chandler was going to the hospital. And I'm not worried about him at all—I know he's going to be okay. I'm not worried, but I'm a little crazy on the inside for a few reasons. Like I mentioned, if I get stressed, my mind goes a little overboard on thinking things, and I can't think straight. When it comes to getting a surprise—any kind of surprise, a good surprise or a bad surprise—it can throw me into that area. And I'm not fully stressed, because I'm speaking perfectly fine, but even still, when I heard about Chandler, my thoughts went a little racy. I felt a little odd in the stomach. I am a little worried about my brother, but I know he'll be okay.

You just described your feelings for your brother. Could you differentiate between thoughtful ideas about your brother and emotional feelings? Is your reaction more in your head or more in your heart?

I'm really not sure how to explain that, because I don't know much of a difference. I would say that it's more in my head. In my heart, I am thinking more about girls. My head is thinking about my brother and my family members, because really my heart needs something better than just family. I'm only kidding. I would say that the weird feeling in my stomach is probably my heart feeling a little bit worried, a little bit surprised about the news. I actually felt that my eyes were watery a tiny bit, so that could be part of my heart—part of me is a little worried. Part of me is also in my head. I guess I'm not particularly worried based on what I've heard from my dad. He said my brother just needed to have his appendix out, that it's not serious. My mind and heart are not fully in a crazed conflict with thoughts and fears and worries about my brother. It's nothing I need to worry about. It's not like my brother is suffering from a really critical disease.

How would you feel if your mom got very sick?

I already know how I would feel, because my mom is not very well. She has diabetes, and when she was a little kid, she had a tick bite, and, unfortunately, she still has the venom from the tick in her body. She tends to be in bed a lot. She has to take not only a shot, but 12 pills in the morning and 12 pills in the afternoon. Sometimes when she wants to go to the movies with me, she starts to feel ill, and then she starts crying because she feels bad that she can't go to the movies with me. I remember I had to cheer her up—I was telling her that we weren't really that interested in the movie. The only reason we were going was because she wanted to go. If she couldn't go, there was no reason for us to go. My mom also has a problem when it comes to strobe lighting and a lot of flashy lights. She can go into a bit of a seizure. And I remember that I witnessed that one time, and I was a little panicky, as well. My mom feels bad that she makes me worried. She doesn't need to be—it's definitely not her fault.

I remember when I was young, my brother and sister and I were not getting along with each other. Sometimes Mom would have to yell at us or discipline us. And, for a person like me who has trouble with yelling and gets headaches, I never liked it. As I got older and so did Katie and Chandler, Mom stopped yelling. But, I remember when it came to the day where she moved away to Maine to start her dream of running a bed and breakfast. I understand why, and I kind of liked the fact that she was doing this. I felt more attached to her when I realized she would be more distanced from me.

When I'm with my mom every day, her problems and flaws upset me. But when she's farther away and I get to just see her for a while, I get more excited to see her, I get happier, and I feel like it really helps me to see her. When it comes to my mom feeling ill, almost every time I meet her, I have a slight feeling of worry. She's asleep sometimes in the car, and I look back sometimes just to check in on how she's doing. I always ask if Mom's okay. I never get upset from this, but the real hard part I wonder about is one day she will be gone. That's a day many kids wish wouldn't happen.

When I look at her and think about how she has to take all these pills and have these operations, I just know that...I always feel like her time is cut slightly shorter. I don't know much about her problems, but knowing how much trouble she has and how much she's going through, I just don't know what to think when it comes to the day she might be gone. Will I be a full-grown man, an adult? Or will I still be a young man when it happens? I am not sure how to cope with it. I know I'll get through it, I guess…I just know it's something everyone has to go through, and one day I'll go through it. This will happen to my dad as well, and I'll have to go through it. But seeing my mom in bed, ill, a lot of times, taking all those pills, it's kind of like showing me a sign. She has less time now than she once did. That part gets to me a lot. I know I have to face it, and I will need to handle it when it happens.

You've spoken about your brother, and now I want to ask how you feel about your sister, Katie.

She is the second youngest in my family. I'm going to admit that she's a little better than she was when she was a kid. I mean, she's still a problem for me, but not as big a problem as when she was young. Today, the one thing that bothers me the most with my sister is that she thinks that she knows what's right for us and behaves like a mom sometimes. And I really wish I could say, "You're one to talk!" I remember one example, from a few days ago—she was going to criticize me because I was going to have a small piece of cake in the morning. Just a little treat. My dad's birthday was a little while ago, and there was some cake left, and I just wanted to have a little treat. She told me that I shouldn't eat cake in the morning, that it's too much sugar, that I'm taking pills, and that I don't work out at all.

She also annoys me by playing loud music. She watches a lot of shows and turns the volume up to max. And you know what annoys me the most? If I show up and say a few words, she'll scream, "Will you shut up?" And that's inexcusable, too.

She has the volume up way high, and yet, she wants everyone to be completely quiet. Especially when she's watching her shows in the living room, right next to the kitchen and the dining area. This is the middle of the house, where everyone walks by. And all I can say is, "Katie, people talk in this area. It's not your private spot. If you want to watch something with perfect quiet, watch it in your room."

Right now she is a bit nicer, and she does do nice things once in a while. And she needs to learn to change her attitude.

Regarding your sister Katie, does she understand you?

I highly doubt that. It feels like she completely forgot anything she knows about me. She aggravates me a lot with this. She's seen my video; she was even in my school, and the schoolteacher showed the class my video, and of course, everyone was looking at her. When I said, "Hey, my name is Alex Olinkiewicz," the kids said to her, "Is that your brother?" Even after the video, she doesn't get it. I don't know what to say about her.

Sometimes she questions me about the way I drink, the way I talk, and the way I eat. And when I tell her "I can't do that," or "I have a problem with that," she just turns away and rolls her eyes at me, with a bad attitude. Sometimes I have to sit at the table; I have to switch chairs so I can feel comfortable. The only problem is that the chair is slightly higher than the table. So, I'm a little bit higher up when I'm sitting at the table to eat my meal. When I'm drinking, I sort of make a swishy sound in my mouth, because I don't just like to swallow, I like to suck on my drink when I take sips. When I talk to myself, she looks at me like I'm a weirdo. This all goes through my mind. Has she forgotten who I am? Maybe that's the case, because she doesn't really seem to care much. I think she just forgets totally.

If she understood me, she wouldn't be looking at me with such odd looks. She wouldn't be rolling her eyes at me when I tell her I can't do this or that. When Liza says, "Oh come on Alex," when I have a problem, or sometimes she rolls her eyes a tiny bit, at least I know she's a friend. And she has a little bit of a problem with me. But at least in the end, Liza usually understands. Sometimes there are things that Liza doesn't understand, because I am not always perfect at explaining things. But my sister, who's been with me for many years—I just don't know what goes on in her head. I think she's just getting more and more obtuse.

Do you think your sister acts out of frustration, or do you think she acts out as a result of a lack of knowledge of your style or your particular way of being?

I don't know about that. I think there are many times she feels angry at school and has problems at school. I could say, "Try to improve yourself." At least I have sort of an excuse as to why I have trouble. And I do have a reason to need to get help. My school was not equipped to handle this disorder. She doesn't have my kind of problems, so there is no reason for her to misbehave. This is why she probably has trouble at school.

What positive steps have you taken to remedy the situation?

I don't try to argue or fight with her. There are moments when I do yell at her a bit, but nothing really serious. I don't call her names—only when she is not around. I don't do that, since I know that if I did, she would try to give it back to me, right then and there. If she gives me a problem, I just call Dad. Even then, she still gets mad. She says, "Alex, you're twenty-one years old, and you're still calling Dad. You are a tattletale." She still tries to do that. She just doesn't want me to tell Dad. She doesn't want to get in trouble. If they don't get into trouble, then almost everyone will go free after doing what they did, and that is wrong. Any time Katie gives me a hard time, I call Dad up and tell him, and have him try to take care of it. Katie tries to get out of it, telling Dad I'm being baby, and all she's doing is trying to prevent herself from getting into trouble. And that's just not going to work.

Is there anything else you've tried?

I don't know if there's anything I can do. I don't say anything rude to her. I try to collect my thoughts at times. I don't say "loser" to her or try to be rude to her. I just say, "Hey Katie, how are you doing?" There are moments when she seems nice. I have to admit, there are random occasions where she seems to be like a good sister. I needed to go to GameStop, and she was going there anyway, so she took me along. And I do help her out with some problems. Like she needed to go off-island,

and her friends weren't around, and she needed someone to be with to make her feel comfortable, so she asked me. And I agreed. We didn't fight at all. We just talked a bit, and that's all. There are moments where she shows signs of good behavior. But that's not saying much, compared to almost every other day.

How would you enlighten her in terms of your Asperger's syndrome and all the things that are part of that? How have you tried to educate her?

I don't want to talk to her about these things, because if I do, she doesn't want to listen. When I try to explain something, she doesn't want to hear it. So I feel like there's no point in my trying. All she's going to do is say, "I don't care, I don't want to hear it," and walk away or something. So there's no point.

Note. By the time this book is finished, my sister will have graduated from high school and will be heading to college. Her behavior lately has improved a lot, and it looks like all my issues that I had with her are gone.

You have an older sister, Brittany, and a younger brother, Chandler. Would you tell us how they came to understand your Asperger's? What problems might they have had, and how have you helped them?

I think you have to talk to them about this. I'll start with my brother first. I'm not sure how he slowly learned to cope with it. Part of it was my video, of course. What do I feel about my brother and how he behaves with me? Unlike Katie, Chandler and I have become good brothers. In the past, being around him was tough; it's the old classic thing. When you're young, and your brother's young, you're going to fight. When you get older, you become more attached to each other, and that's what happened. I became more attached to my brother. My brother tends to help me by trying to hang out with me when I'm alone to ease my discomfort.

Are you uncomfortable when you are alone?

When I have nothing to do, my mind overthinks, or my mind can't think at all. It's like my mind just dies. So, when I have that feeling when my head's all empty, I roll my head around the couch, and I can't think of a word to say. I hang out with my brother a bit; we both play video games, and I must annoy him because I won't shut up about video games, and he's not as much of a gamer as I am. He does have some friends that I'm not really happy around. I'm not sure what it is with them. I don't know if they consider me awesome or cool in some ways because some of them seem to have respect for me, and other times they say things like, "Yeah, you may still be a child on the inside." I may still have childlike behavior inside me, but that childlike behavior is somewhere around the age of 12. And these are teens that have just learned about cursing and the gross-out stuff. I really don't need to hear this. Yes, I'm an adult, but that doesn't mean I have to give an answer to all the questions they ask. I remember my brother apologized once because of how they behaved toward me.

There are some moments with my brother that can go wrong; there are times he ends up getting on the wrong side of me. He does seem to understand that there are problems here and there. I'd say he understands me pretty well—no one understands perfectly, but he does understand and he doesn't fight with me because of those issues.

It's essentially the same thing with my older sister, Brittany. I would say I have more of an attachment with my sister than I do with the rest of my family. I think it's because she's older than me. She's more mature, and we barely fought at all when we were kids. We're more attached to each other, and I would say that when it comes to my older sister, I talk to her the most when it comes to feelings. I'd say that she knows a lot more about me, especially my personal stuff. She does try her best to help me out with my problems. In the past, she didn't fully understand me, because I remember she would tell me things that I should do to fix me up. She cared for me, but she didn't understand how my mind worked. The funny thing is, in the past she would say, "Alex, you are too skinny; you need to eat some more food." And now it's like, "Alex, you're too fat; you need to lose some weight." For God's sake, make up your mind! She doesn't do that anymore. She's always sweet and kind to me, and we enjoy hanging out with each other.

14

My Present
Problems

Chapter 14

What are some of the problems you are having now?

My real problems started just after high school. When I got out of school, I was happy to be free, but there's still that one problem that everyone goes through. And that is, what's next? I have a plan, which is to write these books and stories, but I am still going through a little bit of trouble. Number one, I thought I might try to get a job for a while, or maybe find a college class to attend. However, it's been tough to find a job that fits me. Mostly because:

1. Many jobs around where I live have been taken, and the jobs I might feel comfortable with are too far away from me, and I have a problem with driving. So I can't drive to work.

2. Any job that is near me is not a job I can handle, or it actually bothers me. The same things apply to college classes. I have to find a class that is interesting to me, but there are not a lot of them. And, I already went through 12 or 13 or 14 years of school. I really don't want to have an extra 4 years of my life taken away by going back to school. I have had such a hard time going through school before, that another 4 years would cause some of the same problems I already had.

The biggest issue for me since leaving high school is that I've been almost completely isolated. I'm more isolated than I have ever been. I've been spending most of every single day sitting on the couch, watching the same reruns of shows I've already seen. Or, I play video games. It's been such a boring 2 years. It's been so boring that it's been aggravating me. There's nothing to do, and I've been having cabin fever. That's a phrase for when you're stuck in a cabin, and there's nothing to do, so you just go stir crazy from it. I'm going through that right now.

Another thing that frustrates me is that I can't go out to places. I'm having trouble finding a relationship. This is what I want to have. You know I would like to meet a girl and hang out. But unfortunately, it's been hard to find one. I'm trying some dating sites, and, unfortunately, barely anyone replies to me. I can't even blame my disorder, because one of the things with Asperger's or autism is that people sometimes misunderstand what we are trying to say. And sometimes what we say is considered rude to other people or misleading, when we're just trying to express how we feel. We don't know why this is considered wrong.

15

My Computer

You're very attached to your computer. Can you tell us why?

It's the only connection I have with the outside world. My television and my PlayStation also have a purpose for me. For example, I use the PlayStation to play games to relieve my stress. I watch movies and shows because they're a pleasant distraction. The same goes for my computer. Plus, there are some things a computer can do that a home console can't.

When I'm online, I can find various kinds of news on the Internet. I even use it to look up new game play sales. So, I have some connection to the outside world through my computer. Because of it, I'm not so isolated.

Because I have reading problems, I have trouble getting information from other sources. Yes, a computer does contain text, but it's more simplified. For me, the newspaper is so cluttered with topics and news reports that I get lost in what I see to be clutter. But on a computer, it's basically a search engine where I can find a specific topic that I'm looking for. It's something that really captures my interest.

Although, I must say there are a number of things on the computer that I don't use, which are Facebook, MySpace, and Twitter. Many people go overboard using them. So many products are sold on them that I find it distracting. I actually hate that stuff. I've never had a Twitter account, and I've never had a Facebook account. I am not going to be able to make you my friend on Facebook, because I don't have Facebook.

I think the other reason why I use a computer is because it gives me the ability to be outside of my world, and it's another source to relieve my stress. For example, if nothing is on TV, at least I can go on YouTube and look up something funny to watch. If I'm really stuck in a game and I'm getting frustrated, I can research topics that interest me. Then I can skim the computer for quick help. In some ways, the computer does help me with personal problems. It's another source to relieve my stress.

You called yourself a "gamer"—would you explain to us what that means?

Well, a "gamer" is a person who is fixated on playing video games. I really enjoy video games, and I play them a lot. Some people don't like the word "gamer," any more than you would call people who watch a lot of films "film watchers" or "moviers," or people who read a lot of books "bookers."

However, that's not really what you're asking. You don't really care about why I'm called a gamer. No, I know that's not what you are aiming at. You are asking, "Why I enjoy video games so much and spend so much time playing them?"

The reason why I'm a gamer is the same reason I like cartoons. Games have an added bonus that makes it more enjoyable for me. In a cartoon, it's its own world, its own design its own creation, its own place to be in. A video game is basically the same thing. But there's one thing it has that cartoons don't. It's something you interact with. You actually interact with that world. That is a quality of video games that really shines for me.

I play a lot of games. The best part is that I have the opportunity to interact and explore other worlds. Even if it's simply pressing a button or moving a stick that moves your characters around, you're still having interaction with what's going on in that world. Some video games are very simple: You get from point A to point B. With others, you can tamper with the whole virtual world if you want. It's something I really enjoy. It's a world I can dive right into. I literally have control of the characters and their quest in that world. Even if the outcomes remain the same no matter how many times I play it, I'm still having the experience of throwing myself into that world because I am controlling the characters.

When you were in high school, you were in the library, sitting by a window in the back, away from the tables. Do you recall that?

You could say it was more like a countertop-like setup. For me, the library wasn't the most comfortable place, but it was one of the only places I could be, especially for study hall reasons; and the reason I was sitting at the way edge of the countertop was because I use my own computer. I don't use the school's computer, because it restricts your usage. And, considering that I require my laptop for almost all my needs, I need my own laptop and not the school's.

So, the school's Wi-Fi is locked to prevent anyone who doesn't go to the school, or anyone who brought their own laptop, from messing up the system. It's like a protection they use for their Wi-Fi connection. So, unfortunately, I couldn't really get the Internet at school; however, across the street, there was a house that had Wi-Fi and if I sat in the right spot in the corner of the library, I could actually get a good signal. And I could use that to watch something I liked, or I could go to the sites that I wanted on my computer. I sometimes used that to get on video sites to keep my mind occupied and calm my mind while I watched some funny shows until the next class began.

16

My Psychological Services

Have you ever received psychological therapy or any kind of advice from a professional?

Well, if you mean a psychiatrist or psychologist or whatever you call it, yes, I have, in the past. I don't remember how many psychologists I met, but I saw a lot of them. And then there was one I saw when I was in school, and I called him "Dr D" because his name started with a "D." He was the school psychologist, and I saw him once a week during that time. I came across so many different psychologists. In the end, I never really knew what they did that helped. I just answered their questions. Every question they asked me was the same old question I always used to get.

I know that psychiatrists can help you, but I guess in my case, I didn't really end up needing a psychiatrist. They were just all the same.

You just spoke about the kind of help psychiatrists did or didn't give you. Would you comment on who gave you the greatest advice or influenced your thinking the most?

I don't think any of them really gave me advice that I tried, but they never really were a fit for me. Like I said, I've already seen too many psychiatrists, and I don't even remember one that helped me out. The only psychiatrist I remember the most is Dr D, and that's just because he was someone I saw every week at school. So of course I remember him. When it comes to every other psychiatrist, I don't remember any of the advice they gave me, and I don't remember the things they tried to do for me. All I remember is sitting on the couch staring at the psychiatrist and being asked a question, and I had to say the same things over and over again. I think the only people who gave me advice were not psychiatrists, they were more like friends or family members. You don't always need a psychiatrist to give you advice. You need your friends and family, people that you grew up with and that you trust.

When it came to the psychiatrists I met, they never really felt like friends, which meant I never really felt any of their advice could be helpful. With Dr D, since I spent so much time with him during the school year, of course I kind of had more of a friendship with him. So I guess some of his advice actually did help a bit. But in the end, to be honest, when I'm looking for someone for help, I'm looking for a friend or parent to talk to. They are trustworthy. When you feel there is something to talk about, they're right there for you. You don't need to schedule a talk to be able to talk with your family or friends.

> Based on your past experience, can you remember some of the best advice people gave you?

This is a short answer, but, no, I don't really remember any advice I was given. I don't really recall if anyone gave me much advice. There were some suggestions to help ease my stress, but in the end, most of their advice didn't work. I don't know. I just don't remember much of my life in psychiatry treatment. It was just something that was there, and now it's forgotten.

What about your parents? Or your friends? Do you remember any of their advice?

I think it's just that there are now things in the back of my
head that I never look at deeply enough to remember where
they came from. When you're a child, when you learn how
to speak, it's not in the back of your head, and I don't really
think you can dig deep enough to find out who taught you how
to talk. Was it your mom, or was it your dad? Sometimes when
you get advice, you don't tend to always remember who the
person was who gave you advice. I'm not fully sure. It's completely lost to me right now. Maybe later on, my mind will get
the answer, but for right now it's just something in the back of
my head.

Have you received physical therapy to help you with the
pressure you feel on your feet?

You're talking about for example, if someone had a fear of
snakes, in physical therapy, they try to use fake snakes to try
to get you to touch them so you can build up to real snakes
and get over your fear. Or, for example, they give you a different item to try on your feet to actually help you feel more
comfortable. I might have gone to some physical therapy, but
I'm not really sure. Mostly, it's the same thing with regular
therapy. I don't remember much about any of that, but I can
say that I didn't have much physical therapy.

I see on your table that you have some medications. Can you tell me what they are and why you take them?

One's for my blood pressure, another is an antidepressant, and the others are just vitamin pills to help me get better if I'm feeling a little under the weather.

Alex, a couple weeks ago, you discovered that by tapping your hand or by tapping your fingers on your hand, you became relaxed.

Not 100% relaxed, but it helped distract part of my brain.

Now, I saw that as a change in your physical approach to relaxing your brain. Do you think that you could find another way that may not be as obvious or overt to the public eye that could calm your brain?

I guess so. You never know what might come across your way that helps you out with your issues. There are always the other methods that some people have discovered, like drinking alcohol, which I don't do. But some people go with that. When some people find a better remedy that most people do not do, yet it has helped solve their issues, it may not be acceptable in society. But if it's not hurting anyone, I can go with that.

On a few occasions, I saw you get upset, but I didn't see you do anything out of the ordinary. And I think that's pretty good. What are your thoughts on that? What makes you go into tapping with your hands?

When you see me crying or upset, and you see me down at times, you don't see me tapping, and you don't see me do any of that stuff. There are certain states where I'm actually nervous or almost getting upset, and I actually do it. It's because when I get really upset, my mind tends to shut down. When my mind shuts down, it doesn't think, so my body doesn't do the tapping reactions. Usually the things that upset me tend to make my mind be frozen; it doesn't try to think. And usually the things that distract me are things that cause me to breathe heavily. Those are things that are distracting me from doing my physical relaxers.

When you're upset, your mind is focused on the things that make you upset and the things that are bothering you. You've been in the presence of other kids with Asperger's, and you see them tapping the side of their head or making some strange gestures or noises. How do you compare their way to the way you react?

In a sense, I do the same things they do. I don't tap my head a lot when I'm excited. I don't do weird things like wiggling my fingers, but I do motions with my body to help distract my mind a bit. Anyone with my disorder tends to do that. They always move some part of their body to keep their mind distracted. Some of them do it in different ways, and my way is different from the rest.

What is your advice regarding trying to stop children from doing those things?

Well, if it's not harming him or her, if it's not causing any damage to their bodies, if they're not banging their heads on the wall and giving themselves big bruises, if they're not biting their bodies, if what they're doing is not causing any serious damage to them or the people around them, then you should just let them be calm and comfortable in their world. And if you try to take that away, it will be very difficult for them to handle being in this world. This is what helps them ease themselves, and if it's not causing him or anyone else any trouble, there's no point in making them stop. If it looks weird or obnoxious, well, then so what? The person's not going to care if he's being weird. Let him think that way. It's not a big deal. It's something that's important to him, and nothing else should get in the way of that. If someone does have a recurring quirk that tends to be damaging—something that could really hurt the person—then I do suggest trying to help that person find a different solution that convinces him to do something much safer.

Let's say a kid bites his arm a lot when he gets really sad. Okay, well, in this case, have him nibble on something when he gets upset, instead of biting his arm. He then can bite a piece of candy or something to help keep his mind occupied. Or, for example, if a guy is punching his face a bit too hard that he's getting bruises, try getting him a punching bag or a stress ball, so he can actually put his anger into that. If the kid is doing something that is going to physically hurt him or physically hurt others, then that is something to worry about. But if he is doing something as basic as tapping his hand, or tapping his head, or wiggling his fingers, don't bother. It's not hurting anyone, and it's not hurting him. So let it be. It's what's helping him handle this world.

Do you feel like you've outgrown some of your physical habits?

I may have, but what I have done is substitute replacements. In fact, sometimes I feel like the older I get, the newer and newer habits I gain to help ease myself. You learn some of the new techniques. It takes people a while to learn to start walking, but when they do, it becomes a big part of their lives.

It's the same thing with people who find out in their teenage years that they need to take showers more often and put on deodorant. It's just another new thing they have to do. So, there are new habits that make me feel comfortable, and they may show up and become a new part of my life. Do I lose any habits? No. Do I gain new habits? Most likely, yes. It's just a part of everyone's life.

Occasionally, we have had conversations on the phone, and you are inclined to cut them short or keep them brief. Could you explain why?

I really can't stand talking on the phone. I have a cell phone, but I hate carrying it around, and I hate when I'm really relaxed, and I am suddenly interrupted by a telephone ring. I think it's gone from being an "okay" thing—something that didn't bother me that much—to being a full-blown annoyance. When I was young, there were just basic phones on the walls. You'd walk up to the phone and answer it. But now, cell phones are everywhere, and it annoys me to constantly hear the rings and the long conversations from one person's side, when I can't hear the other person's side.

So I don't know where the conversation's going or what it's about. When it comes to conversations through the phone, I can never really think straight. When I talk with a person, I need to use my hands to show the person what I mean. Maybe it's the same reason that I need someone next to me to get me talking when I do my recordings. I think it's also because when it comes to my dad and his job, he has to be on the cell phone constantly. When you have your father talking on the phone for hours on end to do his job, and you want to talk about something else, it becomes irritating to point of desperation. Cell phones don't give me much of a problem when I'm by myself, but it's still irritating to hear voices over the cell phone. I've developed a very odd reaction when it comes to cell phones. I go crazy. I flinch a lot. I move around a lot.

One time, I was with my dad in the car, and we had to wait for my brother to finish practicing basketball. My dad was on his cell phone. Since the beginning of the phone call, my body had started to shake, and I looked at my father and asked him to get off the phone. When I'm in that environment, and the only thing I'm hearing is this conversation that I'm not a part of, I don't know what's going on, and it just makes me crazy. I tried to get out of the car, and I was still moving around a lot. I started to feel a lot of pressure in my eyes, like I was about to burst into tears. I felt like I wanted to yank my hair out, and I didn't know what to do. When my dad finally got off the phone, it took me a while to calm myself down.

Do you believe kids with Asperger's can give up things "cold turkey"? How would it be for you to give up something like Dr Pepper, pizza, or even your computer?

The answer here is both yes and no. It depends on what it is. It would be hard for me to have my laptop taken away or to not have television for a while. When I used to play on the PlayStation 3, the servers went down completely for a month. So, I experienced the full "cold turkey" of not playing video games on my console.

Here's the problem. Take, for example, a kid who likes specific foods. His parents try to get him to give up what he likes "cold turkey," so they can get him to like other foods. There's a difference here. They're still feeding him. He's just being fed foods he doesn't usually eat. He is eating foods that he either thought he didn't like or he refused to try before. They're basically forcing him to try new things, and eventually he will probably find foods that he does like. So technically, he will solutions and alternatives. And that's not exactly "going cold turkey."

If a person needs something like his computer to get rid of an issue, like a form of discomfort, or if he needs that thing to help ease his pain, it distracts him from his uncomfortable environment. In that case, it's not something you should make him quit.

I play video games to ease my pain, when I feel stressed out. If you took that away from me, during those times when I am in pain, I have nothing to get rid of it. It's still in me, and it's just going to stack up, and up, and up. So, you thought it was a better choice for me to not play, but it's not a better choice.

The same thing goes for a person who has a sort of habit where he's tapping his hands or wrists. If you do not permit him to do so, it's going to make him go ballistic. You're preventing him from distracting his mind and making him feel comfortable in his world. If you know that he doesn't need this specific thing to calm himself, and it's not something in his life that he requires to help ease himself or feel comfortable in this world—if that's the case, then it's okay to quit "cold turkey."

You love your Dr Pepper; in fact, you could probably make a commercial for them, because you like it so much. But the question is, what would you experience if you had to quit "cold turkey"?

When it comes to getting rid of something like Dr Pepper, my reaction would not be that big compared to something like having my computer taken away from me. It depends on the level of comfort it gives me—how much I rely on that item. For Dr Pepper, there are a few problems with it. I can handle not drinking Dr Pepper for a while. There are moments where I would crave one because it's a drink that does comfort and soothe me, but I do have other alternatives that I can use to ease myself. I like pasta, and pasta does relax me with its taste.

When I was young, my mom did this "no soda for a month" thing. Of course, it wasn't 100 percent. When we went out, we had soda, but when we were at home, we weren't allowed to have soda. I was okay most of the time, but I did beg for the soda, because it has a nice taste that I like. I would not want to get rid of Dr Pepper, but I am slowly trying not to drink too much of it. I think I can handle that. But when I need it, I do need it.

17

My Therapy

When did you first get a diagnosis and treatment?

When I was about 6 years old, I went on a little trip with my parents. They didn't tell me why. But they told me I had to see two doctors. They wanted to talk to me and examine me. I was happy, because I knew I was skipping school. And, to be honest, I didn't really like being in school that often. The day was long, though.

At the doctor's office, I sat down with my parents and waited, while two women asked me to come with them. I walked into an empty room. From what I remember, there was a table with three chairs, one on one side and two on the other side, and a few bags with toys and books. It had a plain, carpeted floor, and the wall was one color. It wasn't the kind of a room I preferred to be in. But, it didn't bother me as much as other rooms I'd been in.

The two women asked me a few questions. I answered them simply, and the next thing they wanted me to do was play a game. I decided to go along with it, and I played the game. What they did was to pour a few toys on the table. The toys were different, each in their own way. In fact, they were somewhat random in what they picked out, I believe. One was a G.I. Joe doll, one was a Barbie doll, and there was a fire truck, a spinning top with a spiral picture on the top, and probably some other goodies that I have forgotten. They told me to take the toys that were in front of me and try to come up with a story.

I went with the idea that the Barbie doll and the G.I. Joe were riding along on the fire truck, and they were about to enter a portal, and that portal was the spinning top. That picture of the spiral on the top reminded me of what most people would call a wormhole. What the rest of the story was, I don't quite remember. I remember, for some reason, that the story I created with those toys was important to the doctors.

The next thing they did was hand me a picture book, with no words. I think I've seen this book countless times. It's a book with frogs flying on lily pads, and they float around the city creating mischief and fun. There were no words, and they told me I should come up with how the story goes without looking at the next page. So I began, and I tried to tell my story about what was happening in the picture with the frogs. I seemed to go into great detail in every scene. I tried to come up with something different to fix mistakes I made when I turned the page, and the event had completely changed. I did not really understand this, but I do have to admit, I was enjoying myself.

In the end, the doctors asked me a few more questions. Then asked me to leave, and they wanted to talk to my parents. I sat down to do my homework, which I unfortunately had to do, but at least it was easy. It was just rewriting my thoughts about a cartoon that I had seen on TV. So, it wasn't really that difficult compared to other homework.

While I was doing it, I was waiting, and waiting, and waiting, until finally my parents came back, and I asked them, "What did they tell you?" And they told me that my mind worked differently than others. So, at the time, I realized that my odd behavior was because my mind worked differently from others. I was different from the rest.

A few years later, when I turned 16, I was talking with the school psychologist, who I had seen almost once a week for some time. He told me the name of what I had: Asperger's syndrome. After all these years, I finally realized that what I had actually had a name—Asperger's syndrome. I never really realized that it was a disorder, and I was actually surprised to know I had one. At first, when I heard the name Asperger's syndrome, my mind went through the same thoughts that anyone else would have when they hear that name. Some people actually mistake it as "ass-burger" instead of "Asperger's," and, because of this, it sometimes makes you think of something else. To me, at that time, when I heard it, I pictured it as being a weird type of hamburger disease.

But, really, that wasn't the case. The reason why it's called Asperger's syndrome is because the person that discovered it, his last name was Asperger. So it was decided to name the disorder after him. I had to say, I was surprised to hear a man had such a strange name, which is similar to the oddness of mine, Olinkiewicz. I found it kind of interesting. But what Asperger's syndrome really is, most people really don't know.

Well, can I tell you in the simplest way? Have you ever heard of autism? If you've ever heard of it, you know that it's a very strange disorder, where people are literally in their own worlds. They behave differently than others. They have reactions and various senses that feel different than those of anyone else.

Asperger's is a type of autism. In ways, if you think about it, it is actually half-autistic and half-not; it's on the lower end of the autism scale. I know it's hard to picture it, but think about it as the person is not 100 percent fully autistic, but not 100 percent fully part of "the norm," like everyone else. People with Asperger's have some similarities to a regular person. But, at the same time, they are constantly going through some of the issues that people with autism seem to have. These symptoms make them very confused and make them stand out from the crowd. They also misunderstand other people.

18

My Holidays

During Thanksgiving, a time when you're with your family, and a time when you are very relaxed, I heard that you had an unpleasant experience that brought you to tears. Would you explain what happened and why you reacted?

Where did you get the idea that I'd be comfortable on Thanksgiving? I don't know where you'd get an idea like that. That's Christmas. I hate Thanksgiving, and there are a lot of reasons why. I'll give you five reasons.

1. I have a huge family of about 20 people, maybe even more. They're all crowded up, and they talk about everything. It's extremely noisy, there are a bunch of loud kids and adults, and I get irritated from hearing all their loud noises.

2. When people cook a lot of Thanksgiving food, the food smells. Even after Thanksgiving, there is the garbage smell. There are all these different foods that I don't like the smell, so that bothers me, as well.

3. I don't like any of the foods they serve. There's not a single thing on the table that I like. I'm usually stuck with the same food I usually eat, nothing special compared to any other day. So, not even my taste buds enjoy the experience. It's not savory or amazing food that other people have when they eat a Thanksgiving feast.

4. I'm basically in a crowded room full of displeasing pictures and different objects that I don't really enjoy, and I don't really like seeing them. I'm not really comfortable being in a large family crowd. I don't really prefer

many of the colors in the room, which are basic browns and yellows, since they're typical Thanksgiving colors. Partly it is brown and golden because of fall.

5. I just feel uncomfortable with my feelings. They feel uneasy within me from all this. Basically, all five of my senses are uncomfortable or not in a good mood when it comes to this holiday. Even though other people try to help me be comfortable, I still get upset each year, because there is still all that discomfort. I just hate Thanksgiving, and I was very sensitive that day. And it was a real mood changer.

Alex, why did it bring you to tears? And how long did that last?

Well, it wasn't a long period of crying, and I was fragile at the moment, because I was very uncomfortable. I was uneasy, and things tended to happen that make me crack. On my way home with my dad, we were talking about something I didn't like hearing about. I tried to tell him to stop talking, and he continued, and raised his voice. He didn't think he was yelling, but it felt like he was yelling to me. It made me cry. I was already holding my tears in from just feeling down; I don't know why I felt like that, but Dad just brought in my conduct at the party, and that made me burst into tears. It was a couple minutes before I eased up. It wasn't anything big. I was pretty down, I was fragile, and my dad accidentally triggered the breaking point.

It took me maybe an hour to an hour and a half to recover. I wasn't crying for an hour, but I was trying to ease my breathing and bring it back to normal. Probably, I was having a Dr Pepper to calm myself and I was playing video games, and I was trying to ease myself back to normal, but I was still down.

What are your feelings during Christmastime?

I love Christmas. It's my favorite holiday. Christmas is one of the most cherished holidays in my life. I'm not religious. I'm not religious in the slightest. I'm open to religion, I just haven't experienced it yet. I guess I'm waiting on God to show himself to me. I'm a person who's open to believing, but I'm not fully convinced yet. That's who I am. One of the annoyances I get is when people ask me, "Well, if you're not religious, why do you celebrate Christmas? Christmas is the birth of Jesus." The first reason is I grew up with Christmas. My family was always religious, and they celebrate Christmas. I grew up with Christmas when I was young. Christmas is not something that I want to get rid of. I find it really hard to just let it go. I don't really see a reason why I should not celebrate Christmas.

Secondly, Christmas has been so commercialized, it seems to have much more meaning and reasoning to be celebrated, rather than just the birth of Jesus. If you've seen a bunch of specials or cartoons or movies, not all of them always mention the birth of Jesus as the true meaning of Christmas. Most of them mention that it's about being with family, it's about caring for others no matter who they are, it's about the enjoyment of miracles, it's about celebrating the last month of the year— there are so many different ways of celebrating Christmas. I feel like the reason I celebrate it is not only because of the birth of Jesus, but because it brings joy to a lot of people, and I want to celebrate with them.

Christmas is really something magical. I think that's the reason I like Christmas so much. I don't like Thanksgiving, which is basically a family getting together for a large feast. Christmas tends to hold a lot more meaning. You don't tend to hear a lot of Thanksgiving songs—there are few Thanksgiving songs. You just make sure you have a large turkey, cook it, and make sure you make the other basic, traditional foods that Thanksgiving is supposed to have. But with Christmas, there are so many different things, even before the December 25th. It actually starts on December 1 and continues to the 25th. There's always the Christmas lights, which fill everything with colors. It's always magical to see the plain white stars in the sky. Then there are the colorful stars on trees and homes. There's the snow that reflects and shines in the light, especially with the lights on. There are always those presents under the tree, so even though I don't like a lot of surprises, I do get that craving to know what I'm going to get. The tree is full of colors. I like when they have those round, ball-like ornaments that the Christmas lights shine off of. It looks like there are a bunch of stars in the tree. There are so many things I feel very relaxed about at Christmas. I think the meaning of Christmas helps cheer me up, also. It involves caring for others, and, for a guy like me who feels like an outcast most of time, Christmas feels like a holiday where people feel like including even the outcast in the merriment. And, I guess that stirs up a lot of emotions for me.

I do have to mention that there are things I don't like at Christmas, or around Christmas. For example, my dad uses old Christmas decorations for the tree, which is all right, but some of them have lost some of their pieces. I think there's a teddy bear that's lost its leg, and there's a train that's missing a caboose, but there's still the track, and you can still see the adhesive on the tracks. There are old, homemade ornaments. When we were 5, my dad gave us homemade Christmas ornaments. And, I understand that each ornament is memories, but they're not well taken care of. I guess it kind of makes the tree look like it's filled with junk. I get the reasoning, and I appreciate the reasoning. If the ornaments were preserved really well, like they should be, I wouldn't have a problem. But, considering that they're not really taken care of and they're broken, it really bothers me.

Recently, my dad came up with a good compromise, where he lets me put up these ball ornaments, which helps hide most of the broken ones. It does please part of me. But, it still annoys me that my dad still sticks with these ornaments that are decaying. But, for a father who is so fixated with antiques, I shouldn't be surprised about his using old antiques on trees.

There's the 20 family members who show up on Christmas, but there are still things about Christmas that I enjoy. There are the Christmas specials, there's music, and there are a lot of things I can look at that I enjoy. Yes, there are a few things that bother me, but there are just so many things about Christmas that I like that help me overcome my dislike for holidays. I just love Christmas, and even though I'm not religious, I just can't bear to part with it, because it means a lot to me. And it does mean something special.

My Reaction to
Three Movies

Recently, I watched three movies, whose main characters have autism or Asperger's. So, be warned—this chapter may contain spoilers on the films.

1. "Adam" (2009): A story about a boy with Asperger's, who meets a girl and they form a relationship.
2. "Rain Man" (1988): A classic film about two brothers (one with autism) who go on a cross-country road trip.
3. "Mozart and the Whale" (2005): Two people with Asperger's meet each other and begin dating.

Liza and I just finished watching "Mozart and the Whale." After I saw it, I had some emotional feelings. We discussed these emotions, as well as other movies we saw that gave me similar reactions, such as "Rain Man." Another film we discussed was "Adam," which was similar to "Mozart and the Whale;" the only difference is that only one of the people is autistic, while the other person is not.

Alex, how are you different from each character?

That's a little difficult for me to say, because there are a lot of things I can relate to. First, I should say that all three characters from the three movies are all autistic savants, and they all have a high degree of intelligence.

Adam is extremely knowledgeable about space; he knows all the ways that space works. I would say that he is not much of a savant, but someone who has a strong fixation for space, so he knows a lot about it.

Rain Man, he's fully autistic, but he is tremendously good with numbers. "Mozart and the Whale" is similar. The male protagonist is very good with numbers ... maybe not as good Rain Man, but he can handle them very well.

I can relate to them because of their difficulties in understanding other people. I can understand people a little better, maybe, but I am still unnerved. I still have a hard time understanding what other people are thinking or how they are feeling. The characters in the movies end up breaking down and being terribly upset from something in their lives that has changed or from an unexpected event. It shows that it's not really easy for them to adapt. I can relate to this kind of experience, because I have similar reactions to change in my life. All the characters seem to have a problem with certain noises. They tend to mumble. Some of them actually sway back and forth and don't stand up straight. In all honesty, I can fully relate to them.

But, there are probably a few differences compared to me. One character from the movie "Mozart and the Whale" does what I don't do, and that is, he leaves stuff around. When he walks into a room, he has garbage lying around. He has stacks of newspapers just thrown about. That's where he wants them, and he keeps them that way because any changes might rack his brain. It would wreck his world if the environment were changed. He leaves his materials there because he knows where they are, so he feels comfortable. But once that stuff is cleaned out or removed, he will be lost. Then his mind is searching, "Where did this go? Where did that go? What happened to that?"

You see this when his girlfriend decides to clean up the mess. For him, it is a total surprise and a shock. She has cleaned up everything and organized all his newspapers alphabetically. But the problem is that because he has to have

Chapter 19

everything where it once was, he has a panic attack. Now he wonders where everything is. It's the old classic problem, where he has to know where "that thing" was and where is "it" going to end up. He might go into a panic.

I'm just the opposite. I like things organized and can spot when something is out of order. It upsets me to a degree when my things are disorganized.

Another thing—that character is a pet person. He has birds, and he enjoys talking to his birds. I am not a pet person, so that's another big difference between us.

Rain Man? It's pretty obvious that there is one big thing different between us. He has a much more severe disability... he is extremely autistic compared to me. So, his behavior is stranger. He spends most of his life—in fact, his whole life— in his own world. The outside world is basically unknown to him. So, his behavior and actions are more extreme. But, even still, I still understand him very well, because I do spend time in my own world. I spend parts of my life living in a different world. I do understand what his mind goes through and how he must live every day.

Finally, with Adam, I would say that aside from the fact that he is fixated on space, he is probably the one I can mostly relate to. However, although we are very similar, he doesn't sit Indian style, as I do.

One of the clear signs that we are alike is that Adam has trouble understanding people—more so than I do. He's not that good at socialization. Oftentimes, he says the wrong things. I always feel like I do the same things.

The Three Movies and Me

Can you think of anything else that makes you different
from the three characters you are analyzing?

The only difference I know is that Rain Man lives in a mental
hospital for people with disorders. However, he lives somewhat
independently. He just follows the everyday routine: In the
cafeteria, Tuesday is meatloaf night, and he knows what to do.
He probably gets some help here and there, but he can pretty
much live independently. Outside of that mental hospital, he
can't figure out what to do. Adam and the guy from "Mozart
and the Whale" are both able to live independently. The problem with me is that I'm not capable of doing that. I still find it
surprising how some people can cope with it. They're able to
live on their own, and I'm so handicapped by it.

It's like a comparison between Rain Man and Adam. When
it comes to Rain Man, he is so fixated on his own world—he's
strongly autistic—you can tell he can't live on his own. He has
to live in that hospital or have someone to take care of him.
He can't be by himself at all, because he can't go through life
without help. Adam has some form of autism and has trouble
understanding things and coping with certain things. He does
need a helping hand here and there, but besides that, he is able
to handle some things. He had a job, but when it came to shopping for food, in the beginning, he had a freezer full of maca-
roni and cheese. When it is empty, he runs out, but you don't
see him go to the store and pick up more, probably because he
doesn't know how to cope with going to a grocery store.

When he tries to handle business work and looking for a
new job, he's able to do it with the help of a friend or his girlfriend. A friend of his father helps him a lot on the way. He

is able to live on his own most of the time, but he still needs some help from his friends.

Where am I in that area? Simply put, there's a lot of me that's more like Rain Man, but there's a lot of me that's also like Adam. Because I'm so much more social than they are, people tend to think because I'm so social, I have the least amount of autism. But I have more serious autism than most people think. The only difference is that I'm so social. But, that doesn't mean that I only have a small percentage of autism. If you compare me to Adam, you might think I'm able to do things because I'm so much more social than he is. Just because I'm able to triumph with one thing that people with Asperger's still have trouble learning doesn't mean I have triumphed over everything to the point where I'm not autistic. People misunderstand it.

We've been talking about Adam. At one point, his girlfriend lies to him, and he has a great disappointment and rejection with his relationship. He breaks it off, and he leaves the apartment in a hurry. Now, I regard that as an absolute reaction. Have you experienced any of that?

I feel those reactions when I hear slight lies, and I feel down. But when it comes to odd experiences, when something shows up out of the blue, when something I felt happy about ends up being a disaster, I feel let down. I've had an event or two like that, when something happened that I did not expect to happen. What Adam went through was because he thought he knew the girl, and when he finds out she lied about one thing, he wonders what else she lied about. His mind goes overboard with so many different possibilities that it just makes him go crazy, and I know that I would experience some of the same reactions.

Can you relate to them in terms of their weaknesses? Do you feel that your form of Asperger's is superior to theirs in the way that you can handle yourself?

I am equal to them. They all have different problems that lead up to different conclusions on how they handle life. They have trouble trying to socialize with people. I am able to do that. But they are able to live on their own. I can't. Some of them are able to do mathematical problems in a snap. I can't. They can't really talk to people and give them advice. I can. It's just equal. I can't tell if I'm superior to or weaker than the others. Maybe I could say that I am superior at socializing with people compared to them, but I'm way weaker than them when it comes to trying to find a job. I can't say I am superior to them or weaker than they are. I just have different weaknesses and different strengths compared to them.

Give us some insight into the way you like to be organized.

When something in my life becomes disorganized, it bothers me. It's an irritation. I need things to fit the way that I want them, because if they don't, I just can't think right. It's a distraction. When I'm watching television, and I look up and see those videos lined up on the bookshelf and there's that one video that doesn't fit, I can't stop looking at it. Thoughts start to flow, even if it is a misplaced DVD. People have said to me,

"Dude, it's just a DVD, let it go." But I can't. It sticks out like a sore thumb. For example, a gardener likes to keep his garden organized. If he notices one weed that's stuck in the ground and he has a hard time pulling it out, other people would say it's just a weed, but it bothers the gardener, because it ruins his garden. It's only a small weed, it may not be a big deal, but the gardener wants to get rid of it. He wants it out of his garden. It's just like a sore thumb. It's a distraction. Even if the weed isn't bothering the plants, and it's not doing any harm, he still wants it out of his garden.

Tell us about how your gift is different from the gifts of the characters in the movies.

Adam is not that social compared to me. I have the gift of being social. A lot of people who have my disorder find it very difficult to socialize. Sometimes they do express themselves, and sometimes they do socialize...some do verbalize well enough that you can understand them. At the same time, there are still always things they say incorrectly. There are some things they hear from other people that they don't quite understand. I have the same problem, sometimes. But, again, my way of expressing concepts is superior to others, which enables me in a book like this to express myself.

Giftwise, the difference is pretty obvious. When it comes to Rain Man and the character in "Mozart and the Whale," their common gift is that they are pros at math. They're almost like human calculators. You literally give them a math question, and they are able to give you the answer right away. Adam is extremely intelligent when it comes to space. He's just so fixated and fascinated by it, and he learns so much about it. That's his gift.

Me, I am actually very gifted in expressing my inner self to the outside world. It is rare for a person with Asperger's to be able to do that. Parents and psychologists find it hard to understand the autistic mind. That's because it's been so difficult for a person with autism to explain their symptoms. The combination of a person who has autism and who can articulate the internal workings of his mind is my gift.

It's an original gift. Everyone else takes the understanding of his or her mind for granted. For someone like me, it's sort of an achievement. Even if I still have problems in dealing with my mind, it's still an achievement.

Tell us about your organizational skills.

There's always different ways that people organize things, especially people like me, who have my disorder. I organize things differently for other reasons. There are people with Asperger's who leave stuff wherever they drop it, mostly in stacks, and they only move the stacks when they really need to. They always have to leave things where it seems convenient, but they remember where they left their things. They can't move them around too much, or they lose track of things and get very upset.

Other people like to have specific things in a specific order. With me, it's sort of a mix. I like to have things clean. I like to have things sort of even. You could say that I have a bit of symmetry in me. I like the look of symmetry. If you look at my shelves, you will notice that they are balanced. There are two books from the top that are the same size; one on the left, one on the right, and in the middle is a box. You probably notice that below it is a book, a couple of movies, and a couple of book markers, holding them in the middle. There's a toy on the left side...actually an action figure on the left side and a plushy on the other side, to even things out. Below that, you'll also notice that I have my video games on one side and my blue-ray movies on the other side. I also have three statues in the center. It's not that I'm into symmetry fully—I don't need perfect symmetry. What I need to calm my mind is something that evens things out.

I can always tell if something is not in the center. When I look at things and they are not in their proper place, it bothers me. For example, I like video games, and I have a PlayStation 3. When you look at the spine of the game case, it has the company's logo in red on top. But, when they made a new model, which is the slim version, they actually changed the font to give it a more classic look. So now it disturbs my sense of symmetry. The new bookends have a slightly larger black area, with a weird white text that says 'PS3.' Because of this, I find it distracting that the logos don't match each other. This imbalance disturbs me.

But, I've found a solution. Luckily, some of the games that had the original logo were re-released as greatest hits. What this means is that they've been re-released with the games with the new logo. So, I decided to buy the re-released copies, and now all the logos match.

Before   After

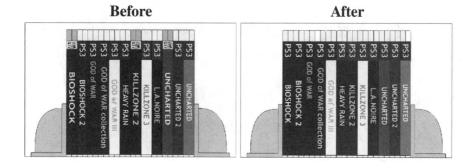

1

A Conversation with Liza

A discussion with Liza, who is both a friend and hired companion for Alex

What is Liza like?

ALEX: She's originally from Guatemala, and she wants to be a psychiatrist or in a related type of field. It's kind of hard to describe her. I'm not really good at describing people. But, I can say it in a simple phrase: Liza's sweet and nice, and she has her own troubles, just like everyone else. She seems to be very caring. Sometimes she's very strong, and other times, she's a bit fragile. Oh, and she's very pretty.

LIZA: You're boosting my self-esteem right now!

ALEX: Well, you know, you keep on complaining about how you look, and I'm telling you that you look pretty fine.

How did Liza come to work for you?

ALEX: My father hired her to help me out. She drives me around, and we watch movies together.

LIZA: Alex, speaking of movies, how did you feel after watching the movie "Adam"? I could tell you felt a little uncomfortable, and ready to cry. What kind of emotions do you feel, and how did you feel after watching the movie?

ALEX: I don't know how I would describe it. In some ways, it was a strong emotional feeling. A feeling that got to me. Because it was something I could relate to. There are things I can understand, and it's a mystery to me how I come to understand. And I guess in some ways, it makes my mind flow with all my past emotions and my past feelings and how I feel toward the characters in the film.

LIZA: It's like you feel that you identify with them—like you're one of them sometimes?

ALEX: I'm not sure what the reason might be. Maybe the reason is that it's almost like I'm watching parts of my life. Sure, I have never been in a relationship as in "Adam," and I didn't go overly crazy on a road trip like Rain Man; but those things, those touches, have happened to me. They are very similar to what happens in the movies. So, it's like I'm reliving a past experience. It reminds me about the kind of person I am. I'm not fully sure, but maybe that's the reason.

LIZA: In the movie "Adam," a nonautistic person is dealing with an autistic person, and they didn't end up together. I remember your crying a lot. Your reaction was a very different one from the movie we saw today, where two characters with Asperger's actually stayed together. And you really didn't cry; you looked affected, but not like you did with the other movies. Do you think this has something to do with you? Like it kind of gives you the idea that this could be you. Why do you feel like you had a different reaction toward this movie?

ALEX: I think part of the reason is that the quality of the films matters, as well. You'll admit it, you and I really enjoyed "Adam." When you watched "Mozart and the Whale," you were a little bored by it. So, it could also be that one had a stronger effect than the other, because it was better made than the other film. But, I think the other reason for that would be that it fits the relationship that I'm hoping to look for someday. For me, I would really prefer to find someone who doesn't have my disability. In some ways, I know I can relate to that person, but the one they showed in "Mozart and the Whale," they showed that the couple had the same problems. I see why I might have a hard time trying to handle being with someone who has my disorder. Because, as you saw in "Mozart and the Whale," they were going back and forth with different upsets and idiosyncrasies. I feel that's why I was upset—fearing being in a relationship with somebody who has the same disorder.

I think I felt more upset with "Adam." It is because Adam kind of resembled me more than the characters in "Mozart and the Whale." And I think that's what really pulled me in. The movie dealt with a relationship where a person who doesn't fully understand Asperger's tries to cope with Adam and tries to understand him.

I think you misunderstood why I was crying. The truth is, I wasn't crying because they broke up. I wasn't upset that they broke up. That part I actually liked a bit, because it wasn't that old, classic, happy-ending thing.

We always predict that the person is going to find the lover, and they are always going to get back together. But, this movie took the risk to have them not get back together. And, I understand that's a part of life. I wasn't upset because it was a sign that anyone who has Asperger's or any form of autism is never going to have a long relationship. No. That's not what went through my mind when I saw the ending of that film.

I think what upset me was just how much I was relating to this character. And I think how I feel toward the fact that the movie had a pretty decent ending. It wasn't an ending where he broke down. It wasn't really a sad ending, because it did show that he learned from some of the mistakes he made in the past. He never thought about asking for help. Thanks to the girl, he had a relationship; he was able to at least learn a few new things to make him more capable to be around people.

I think this was part of the message of the movie. In any case, I think the main point is that I feel that I relate to him a lot more than the character in "Mozart and the Whale." And that's why I felt more emotional.

Liza, what was it in "Mozart and the Whale" that you thought was a little confusing, and I'll try to give you the answer?

LIZA: I definitely saw a lot of things in the movie that I can see in you.

ALEX: Remember, in "Mozart and the Whale," she may have only referenced the disorder, but that doesn't necessarily mean it's the only thing that bothered her. Still, there are many things that bother me. After I viewed the films, they reminded me about one thing that I think most people don't understand. When it comes to most people, when they hear about me having a disorder, they are confused. They think because I am so able to explain how I can emote and be very social, that I have the lowest form of Asperger's or that I'm only a tiny bit autistic—I hear that a lot from other people.

LIZA: Probably people think that your Asperger's is the mildest form.

ALEX: No, no, no, it's not the mildest. It's just somewhere on the spectrum. I do not have the lowest form.

LIZA: There are a lot of people with Asperger's who have been able to explain and help people understand how their minds work.

ALEX: I think in some ways, when it comes to some people, they think I'm not as severe because of how social I am. But I think they forget that when you have one upside, you still have a downside. I think it's sort of a balance. Anyone who has this disorder has a bit of a balance. If you get rid of one problem that other people have, it's replaced with another problem to keep it balanced. So far, I haven't heard or seen a lot of information about people who would sit in an Indian style, or do other things that I do. And a lot of them show they are able to do a lot of things that I can't. Some of them actually have a job. They can drive and are not bothered by noise. But those things are difficult for me.

LIZA: Do you think that those people have a little bit less of a problem?

ALEX: No, what I think is that they have their own downsides, as well as their upsides that actually work for them. For me, my upside is that I am more social with people: I am able to really explain what it's like inside my head. I'm able to look them in the eye pretty well, most of the time, and really give them an insight about what's going through my head. But, unfortunately, since that's my upside, I do have my downsides, which make me feel that I'm more disabled than others.

22

Driving

Why is driving something you can't do?

I can't handle driving; I can't drive at all. And it's not just because I need to sit Indian style, it's also because the way the roads are so unpredictable. And, somehow, I feel concerned that I can't multitask. When people drive a car, they don't stare at the monitors or meters; they stare at the road, and they only glance a few times at the speedometer.

But for me, I would probably be very distracted by both things. One slight thing that might be a small mistake could make me get all nervous and worried. They always say you have to slow down a certain distance from the stop sign. When I'd do it, I would always be constantly asking, "Did I do that right? Was that proper?" and if something happens, like if someone honks a horn, or if someone shouts at me, or something uncomfortable comes out of the blue, I don't know how I would react to that if I were behind the wheel. Even though experts might solve the problem of my Indian-style sitting with handicap tools, there are other things that might give me a hard time.

Plus, I'm terrible—really, really terrible—at directions. I've lived on this island for more than 20 years. I was born on this island, and now I'm a grown-up, and I barely know where I'm supposed to go. I know I'm supposed to go from this road, to that road, to this road, to get to this area. I just remember left, right, left, right, a pattern, but if you asked me for the street name, I don't know it!

Why do you feel that you do not have a good sense of direction?

I'm not exactly terrible at directions. If you point and tell me to go left and go right, I'm bound, hopefully, to find where I need to go. But when it comes to trying to tell me which streets I'm on, it's never something that stays in my head.

I'm not a person that's good at remembering names. When I'm with a person many times, his or her name fixates in my head perfectly so that I can remember it, but when it comes to something like a road or a street, I can't keep that in my head. It's because some things aren't really fixed into my mind like others. In the end, once I hear it, it will sooner or later disappear in my head, and I still lose forms of direction. It would have to be something I must remember. I couldn't forget it. Because my house is where I live, and I've been going to my house every day, I can say the street name perfectly. It's like a man leaving his home and going to work every day to his office building. He remembers the way by route.

But if I were that man and the road was blocked or detoured, I could not find my way. I would not know which way to turn or what direction I was heading.

When it comes to going a far distance on the island, even if it's a place I've been a couple of times, I can get very confused. When it comes to a few turns in the road that I've done so many times, I can actually remember it. But the rarer I see the turns and roads, the less I know them. If you tell me that I could drive myself off the island to GameStop, I would not be able to figure out where I'm going. I've gone there so many times, but I still don't know exactly what directions to take or what roads to turn on. Once I recognize a specific road that I know is different compared to the other roads, then I might remember what direction I need to take. But otherwise, I'm completely lost. It's the same thing when it comes to names. When it comes to roads, they all look the same to me. I'm seeing the same roads, I'm seeing the same trees, and there are only a few different things that help me know where I am. But when it comes to those large stretches of road that all look the same, I don't know when I'm supposed to turn, or the distances or amounts of time I'm supposed to go on each one.

My Personal
Improvement

Looking back on your life, do you recall areas in which you could have improved yourself?

That is a bit of a difficult question, because in the early years, I did not see myself as different, and at times, I lived in a different world. I realize now that I was out of the norm. People around me began to handle me so that I was comfortable. Over time, people helped me see that the way I was acting was not regularly accepted. I remember times when I acted incorrectly or unnaturally. I was unaware what love meant, and I knew the difference between a lover and a friend. I still have issues with this, I know I've made stupid mistake. Some of my old mistakes I have blocked out of my mind.

I can remember when I was young, I was talking to a girl and impulsively gave her a kiss. I didn't know what kissing could mean. I also said things I should have left unsaid. I would ask a girl out and would be rejected. I would be embarrassed, and I didn't consider that she might have a boyfriend. I was embarrassed and should have thought things out. I even tried to rehearse the words that I thought I should have said. I messed up my relationships with my awkwardness when I tried to be with someone special.

Have you become too dependent on your dad? Has this trait become part of your character?

That is something I have to deal with. I look at it this way. Blind people have Braille to help them see. The deaf have hearing aids; the crippled have wheelchairs. For me, I need a person to help me navigate the world. A person is my Braille, my hearing aid, my wheelchair. My solution is that I need a person to navigate the world I live in. In some ways, I am like a young child who needs to climb up on a chair. It's his dad who has to help him onto the chair.

As you look to the future, people will go their different ways. How do you plan to deal with this?

This is a tough question. Most people have their path in life planned as the years go on. I am unable to set up a plan; right now my life and future are disjointed and unknown. I'm scared, like the time when I was caught alone in my basement during a hurricane. My dad and brother and sisters were at my grandmother's house. Our house was without power. I didn't know how to handle it. I panicked. I got into a fetal position. I got upset. I needed someone to help me through this tough experience. Somehow I got up and wandered the streets, not knowing which direction to take. This is one of my limitations. I have a poor sense of direction. Eventually, I found my way, stumbling and crying, searching for my father until I found my grandmother's house. I was about 19 when this occurred. So I need a person. I have to have a person to understand and aid me.

Would you be willing to talk to someone to give you hope, a career path, and a sense of direction? Someone to help you cope?

I have already spoken with psychiatrists. My parents and relatives have spoken with me. The issue for me is that few people understand the world I live in. They don't understand the problems I have, and they try to superimpose their world on mine. No one has found a solution for me. Hopefully, this book will help people understand my world. I am looking for some consideration, and perhaps the real world has to accommodate me. If others do modify their world and understand mine and come to accept people like me as we are, it will be a lot easier for us.

Are you willing to keep searching for your path?

In the real world, everyone is searching. We all search for the right path, the right answer. Mine is just harder to find.

24

My Hope for
the Future

What would you like to see in your future? What are you moving toward in the future?

I guess, simply put, I want to follow many paths in life. I hope to reach the end of a path that I've been trying to achieve. When you want to achieve something, you always have to take a path, and it's not a simple, straight path. It's always rocky; it's always zigzagging; there are always some turns. I just hope that I reach my path very soon, rather than taking the same path the rest of my life. Probably, when I reach the end of that path, I will discover that there's another new path. At least I'll be able to say that I accomplished this path, and I hope to be able to continue on to the next best thing.

There are a couple of paths I'm taking, and I don't really care much about whatever happens in the future, as long as I get there.

Could you describe some of those paths?

Well the path of writing this book ... like actually completing it and seeing what I have accomplished and achieved in this world. I like the path of helping people. *I would like to go down the path of finally getting a girlfriend.* And possibly, finally being able to make enough money to live on my own. (Maybe I will become wealthy after writing this book...you don't have to put that in the book.) I want to finally be able to make enough money to not only be able to live on my own but to be able to hire some people to help me out on certain occasions with certain issues and problems: like a maid or chauffeur. I know it sounds a little crazy, a little too much in some ways. You never know what is going to happen.

What are the other paths are you taking?

Well, one of my biggest hobbies, in addition to being such a good speaker, relates to what's going on in my head. I also seem to have a pretty creative imagination. People say I'm not that creative, but you know, it's debatable. What I like about my stories is that it is awesome to create my worlds and then express my worlds to the "real" world.

When it comes to cartoons and science fiction, they are all different worlds created by one person. And I think the reason why I like to create my own stories is that I like to create my own world. So I know that my work will require effort. It has to be fully made. It has to be fully believable. It has to be something that people want to see. And so, I do have a strong determination to produce my stories. And I do know that when some stories don't work, they either die or in fact, grow into something wonderful.

Most of my stories that I imagine, I haven't even begun writing. Most of them are simple little notes. The reason why is that I want them to be just right. I don't want them to be lazily done. I don't want them to be something I've written quickly, so they will make a quick buck. These are stories I want to make sense. I want them to be portrayed to the audience properly. I want them to feel like there's actually a lot of heart put into this work. So, I'm very fixated on my other world, and I like to express and show it in the best way I know. When I create these worlds, I want the proper venue for them to be expressed.

I have a number of stories in the planning stage, each requiring a different venue.

One such story, which is a horror story, will definitely get to be a film one day. It's a good ghost story, like one told around a campfire or on TV, when you're watching in bed with the lights on, afraid to fall asleep. I know the proper atmosphere for a horror story.

Another story I'm working on is action packed and well constructed. I definitely know that it should be an animated series.

And there's a third one, which is very intense and action packed, not so much creative, but there is so much in it that an audience has to interact within the story. It will be a video game someday.

I know what kind of medium I want my stories to be in—basically any genre. It all depends on what story passes through my mind, what world shines through my head. In the future, I know that I want to be a writer and creator of various kinds of fiction.

How do you remember the different plots and stories that you invent in your mind?

This is really easy. I just remember them. I cannot forget my work. Almost everything I think of, almost every story I come up with that I have a strong passion toward, stays in my head pretty well. I write a few notes here and there about the story sometimes, and there are moments where I'll get out the recorder and record my stories. But honestly, I let all of my thoughts stay in my head, because my head never forgets my creative ideas. The only way I could lose these creative ideas is if I somehow got amnesia. But that won't happen. My stories just stay in my head, and that keeps a lot of people from stealing my ideas.

Part III

Alex's Support System

25

My Father

A discussion with Jim, Alex's father

Jim, does Alex get psychological counseling?

I have taken Alex a couple of times for psychological counseling. The thing is that Alex has a great understanding of his needs, of autism and Asperger's syndrome. The psychiatrists and psychologists who spoke to him were amazed at his analytical skills and self-awareness and believed he really didn't need continued counseling, so we never continued.

What are your long-range plans for Alex? Are there any obstacles in the way?

The long-range plan for Alex is that as he matures over time, he will become more self-sufficient, get a job, enjoy everything else associated with adulthood, and have a happy life. He will still have a difficult time in life, as other people do not understand him. Alex is not the problem. Everybody else who is small-minded is the problem—they have an inability or unwillingness to understand.

The complexities of the autistic mind are not easy to understand. Children with autism may well be the next generation of those who have superior intelligence. They have special gifts that go well beyond the norm. They can easily be the next evolution in life, with their intelligence and sensitivity. You never see them bully, lie to get ahead, or push their way ahead. Their life is pure. We are nowhere near them.

If you had to do it over again, what would you do differently?

That's a hard question to answer. I probably would have pushed the school harder for things that were more pertinent for my son. I would like to have seen more training in preparing him for life after school, to be more capable to face the challenges of the future. This failing is not only common to Shelter Island for children like Alex, it is pretty common in most schools that do not provide the accommodations needed for transitional services.

I tried to allow Alex to be himself, to grow up in a comfortable world where he felt secure and trusted his parents. I wanted to give him a nurturing, understanding, and caring environment. That's what he needed most.

What has been your guiding principle in helping Alex?

I tried to let him be what he is and not push him into the competitive world. I tried to give him his own independence. Of course, he still depends on me. I would like Alex to go shopping, purchase things at the grocery store, and drive. He does depend on me for these things, because there are only certain things autistic people can do. He depends on me because he needs people he can trust. We all need people in our lives we can trust. I depend on my wife, because she respects me and cares for me. We all need trust. Autistic children need it more, and it is an area of understanding many people know nothing about.

Alex has a lot of great insights. One of the things Alex has a solution for is the way teachers teach. He said that if there were 30 kids in the class and the teacher instructed them one day a month in the way that he learns, they would have a real understanding of how difficult it is for him to learn. Let them try to figure it out.

In many instances, teachers, kids, and others do not understand the workings of the autistic mind. It is like any handicap; it's also like racial equality or gay equality. People can be closed-minded. It's the world's perception that must change, so that others come to understand and appreciate those outside "the norm."

Finally, could you comment on Alex's early years and the problems relating to his upbringing?

Whether I want to admit it or not, and or whether my ex-wife wants to admit it or not, having a special-needs child puts a tremendous amount of pressure on a relationship. And many people with special-needs children end up getting a divorce, because one parent understands the child better than the other; one is able to handle the child better than the other, and they fight over it. And that's not the total reasoning for my divorce, but it definitely added to the pressures on us, which then caused other situations to occur because of those pressures.

With a special-needs kid—with Alex—you have to throw out the parenting handbook. To anyone who says, "You have to do this" or "You should do that" or "You should treat your child this way" or "You should not give into him or not help him," that's all malarkey. Those people are not in the situation. They're not living it, and they do not understand it. Many of the things that your parents try to teach you or that you believe is right or that others try to tell you...are wrong. You need to do what you need to do to move your child along in a positive, loving, and caring atmosphere. It's hard enough at times to be able to converse with him or to be able to interact with him, because most of the time, Alex wanted to be all by himself. I always thought it was something I was doing wrong, and I would force him to be in the family and join in all the activities.

I can remember when Alex was young; I would bring him and drag him around to the national parks with all the other kids. He hated it. He got so upset and cried—you'd think that you were tearing the kid's fingernails out. I didn't realize that it was like tearing his fingernails out. I didn't take into account that maybe there are other things going on with him that made these experiences intolerable.

What does Alex have? Autism, or Asperger's? Is it a special need? Is it a handicap? Is it high-functioning Asperger's? Is that the next evolution of humans, as a society and a race? With all of the new electronics and all of the new medical advances coming out, is a new race evolving? And, are these children the cutting-edge involvement of people that are super smart and understand and are in much better touch with their environment? We think that they have special needs, but maybe they're leaving us behind. People don't think that way. People think that this is a problem that I have, or this has become a hindrance to me.

Does Alex need extra help? Sure. Does Alex need me around? Sure. Does Alex have special problems and need special assistance? Without a doubt. Would I change it? Probably not. If I had the chance, it wouldn't even be a decision. If someone told me Alex could be just like everybody else, no, I wouldn't change him at all. There have been many times that I've spoken to Alex, and he's taught me so much about things and thoughts and reactions and interactions that I would have let pass by. I've found that you only need yourself and the people that love you. And that's the hardest thing for people to learn. It's also the hardest thing for people that have a special-needs child to understand.

This past weekend, I was away with my father and a friend of ours. And we went to a McDonald's down in Pennsylvania, and there was a girl having difficulty at the cash register. We were there early in the morning, and there was no one else there, and she was trying. She was trying to figure out how to enter our pancakes on the register, and how we wanted our coffee and teas. And she was having a really difficult time with it. As she worked her way through it, the other girl helped her and encouraged her. And then we got our food, and it took a long time, and we were the only ones in there. It was only supposed to take a few seconds, and my tea was wrong; my friend's coffee was not exactly right. He said, "It's ridiculous...we come in here, and they need to have someone at the counter that gets it right." This is my friend who's been around Alex his whole life. He ended his complaints by saying, "Don't you think so?"

I said to him that I was appalled. And he said, "What do you mean?" I said, "You too have a special-needs niece, a child who has difficulty with things, and waiting a couple extra seconds for your tea or having your tea come out a little bit wrong—it doesn't matter. I'm just ecstatic to see that person in here, trying to work, trying to do the job." I said, "You're part of the problem. They're not part of the problem. You're like the guy who gave Alex a hard time at the gas station for ringing up his order wrong three times. And then he insulted Alex, and now Alex won't work there again. It's not that you're exactly the same guy, but you're here at McDonald's, acting like the guy that gave Alex a hard time at the gas station. If you had said something to the girl, if you had gone up there and encouraged her, this special-needs girl, we would all be better off. She is trying her hardest, at the slowest time of day at McDonald's, so she can learn, and maybe have a better life. I'll stand there for 2 days and wait for that cup of tea. But unless you're part of that understanding, you just don't get it." That was a very emotional conversation, and I was actually teary-eyed thinking about it, because it hit so close to home.

For example, when you're at a grocery store and a kid is having a problem and acting out, and people are saying, "That mother should really take care of that kid" it's not our place to judge. It's not our place to make a decision on her conduct. We're not in that person's shoes; we don't understand if the kid has special needs or not. We all learn in different ways. We all understand in different ways. We are all born differently. And who's to judge that? Who's to say there's something wrong with that kid? That's where I take offense. I take a huge offense. The other day I was coming home from work, and on the radio, there was an advertisement for an autistic Asperger's walk on Long Island. And the leading line was, "Every 18 seconds, a family is devastated by the fact that they've just learned their child has autism or Asperger's." And I said to myself, what is wrong with us as a people? Yes, there is severe autism, and there are people far more severe than my son, and I understand that, but there are thousands upon thousands of us who believe it's a gift. We as a society don't think in the right terminology. We're closed-minded; we don't get it. And until we do get it, it's not going to work. It's not going to be correct. People are not going to understand. Like I said, you have to throw out the handbook. Alex has taught me that on many occasions.

We didn't get Alex tested until he was 8 or 9; maybe even 10. We kept him mainstreamed in school; he had a bit of difficulty. When Alex was small—2, 3, and 4—he always wanted to be by himself. He didn't talk much. He didn't start talking until about 3 or 3½. He always wanted to sit by himself and play with his blocks and toys. I remember he used to love to watch television and interact, and that was his thing. I remember about 15 years ago, in the summer, Alex was inside, and all of the other kids were outside playing. They were all running around, and Alex just didn't want to go out. I took him out, crying and screaming.

If I took him out on another occasion, and it was quiet outside, and it was calm, he would go play by himself. But he didn't want to be with the other kids. I would take him out anyway, and I'd make him go out, and he would start running and playing a little bit, and doing his best. And all he wanted to do was be inside by himself. He was always very awkward with running and trying to be athletic. He would beg me to leave him inside to watch television and play games, but I wouldn't listen. So he was running outside, haphazardly and awkwardly, and he walked almost duck footed—his knees were spread wide, so he ran, not weirdly, but just the way Alex ran.

He tripped and went flying forward, and he landed on his shoulder, and he got hurt pretty bad. And he was holding his arm, and holding his shoulder, and crying, and I come running outside and said, "What's wrong?" He said, "I fell, I hurt, I hurt." He was so upset, and I thought he was kidding. I took him to the doctor, and he had broken his collarbone. And the doctor said to me, "Well, that's the end of his summer, he's going to have to sit inside and watch TV for the rest of the summer." It's funny how the world works its own wonders. This was the beginning of July, and he wound up just having to sit and do what he wanted to do anyway. It was causing him pain to go outside and play, so he wound up falling and breaking his collarbone.

There are so many stories, so many issues we had, so many fights we had to fight. We didn't realize it at the time.

Shelter Island School was good for Alex, but they pushed him to graduate at 18. As a single father who was taking care of Alex, I didn't realize that I could have forced the school to keep him until 21; it's the New York state law. And those 3 extra years, from a maturity standpoint, for a kid with Asperger's, would have meant a lot. He's still like a 12-year-old child 85 percent of the time. And the other 15 to 20 percent of the time, he's a 21-year-old man. But not realizing how much good that extra schooling would have done for him, I didn't request it. Maybe he would have had a better focus to try college or do something later in his life. But he hasn't wanted to go to college, and he wants to do this book with Dr O'Connell, as he so kindly offered. He's always wanted to write books, in his own way. And he'll find his way, if he has people like Dr O'Connell to help him. I believe that all kids and most people find their way. The rest of us as a society have to understand them.

We had issues with school; there were so many. One that sticks out was when Alex was in tenth or eleventh grade—

and I kept Alex mainstreamed in classes. I fought to have Alex mainstreamed as much as possible. The school was actually pretty good about that. They had an aide to go around with him.

In one case, after about a month of school, Alex comes home saying, "I'm having a hard time paying attention." And I said, "Well, aren't you sitting up at the front of the class?" And he said, "Well, I am in a couple of classes, but in English and social studies, I sit on the side of the classroom. They put me at a table where I can sit Indian style." Alex has to sit Indian style because he has very sensitive, tactile feelings in his hands and feet, so it's very difficult for him to stand for very long periods of time. He has to sit Indian style.

I found out from Alex after quizzing him for 5 minutes that he wasn't even facing the front of the classroom. He was sitting at a table along a side wall of the classroom, and he was facing the wall—the teacher was at a 90-degree angle to him at the blackboard. So he had to try and spin on the chair to watch, and even though he didn't take anywhere near decent notes, he couldn't even try to take notes, and the aide was sitting with him. So instead of keeping Alex as part of the class, his teacher put him on the outside of the class. Even though he was in the same classroom, he was not one of the students.

When I heard that, I went up to the school. I was asking them, "What's going on, and why is this happening?" And they told me that they were trying to order special desks for Alex, as they had tried once or twice at the end of last year.

When the desks hadn't come in for the spring session, I went into Alex's room, and as Alex said, there was a table and a chair facing the wall, and the teacher was teaching up front, and the other kids' desks were 15 or 20 feet from Alex's, and they were all sitting together. So in that case, the whole idea of mainstreaming Alex was for nothing, because he was not being mainstreamed; he was not amongst the other kids. Alex should have been in the center, with all the kids around him, so that he felt like a part of the class.

I asked Alex, and he said that he did okay with the desks in the science lab. The desks in the social studies room and the English room had a metal bar that he couldn't get out of, so the desks were getting in the way of Alex sitting Indian style. In the science room, they didn't have a bar on either side, so if they spilled something, the kids could get out of the way on either side. The school kept telling me that they had ordered the special desk, and it hadn't come in yet. I walked out of the special-education room. I walked into the science classroom. I grabbed two science desks and dragged them out of the science room. I put one into the English room, and one into the social studies room, and I said, "Those are Alex's desks. Put them in the center, with the rest of the kids." So in an educated school system, with 75 teachers and special-education teachers who had umpteen teaching degrees, nobody else thought of doing what I did. For 10 months, my son was looking at the wall rather than being a part of the classroom. That's what has to change.

Alex and I have had many talks about different topics. And the one thing that has floored me is that he's taught me so much. I'd never change him. He has taught me that he learns in a different way. "You know, Dad, I learn a certain way. And I don't learn the same way as everyone else. But if we're really going to say that everybody's equal, if there are 30 kids in the class, and I learn one way, and 29 kids learn the other way, then for 29 days, they should be taught the way that they learn. However, for one day a month, they should be taught my way, and then they would have to figure it out." And I sat there, and I took it in, and I was blown away by that insight. His whole thought process is amazing. Just think about it. Wouldn't it be nice if people could understand that concept?

I had many problems with the school system, and many were not that bad, but people don't always think. The biggest thing I found with 29 percent of schoolteachers is that they have tunnel vision. They're in their world. All they know is what they think they know. They're not willing to step outside and figure something else out.

There are only two people in Shelter Island School who did that for Alex. One was a special-education speech teacher, Mrs Weeder, and the other was Alex's godsend, Mrs Anderson. She understood him, she got it, and she knew it. A couple of Alex's aides came pretty close, but it's hard. The problem is that the school had its own ideas. He had to go to debate class, and every time Alex came out of that class, he felt like somebody was stabbing him to death. He was sobbing. He couldn't stand all the noise. It took a while, but we got him out of that course.

When Alex went to school, we realized there was an issue. Alex would go off by himself. Everybody else would be playing out in the yard. There was an old play pole in the recess area. And Alex walked around the pole, in a circle. He walked around the pole because he had to be outside for recess. They wouldn't let him be inside at recess because it wasn't the norm, so he was forced outside, which really bothered him. He was able to adapt, and so what he did was walk around this pole. Day after day, for 40 minutes at recess, he wore a track into the ground and killed all the grass around the pole. If you ever stopped him and asked what he was doing, he'd say, "Oh

I'm thinking. They're forcing me to be out here, so I'm thinking. Because I'm not allowed to just sit there and think. I have
to be up and doing something, because it's recess and I have to
be playing or doing something. So I walk in a circle."

You say to yourself, "Holy cow, this kid with all these tactile problems with his feet and his hands is forced to do this."
Maybe it was a good thing, maybe it was a bad thing, maybe I
coddle him a little bit, but you throw the parenting handbook
out. Because whatever happens, it's all new every day. They
wanted Alex to stand for the Pledge of Allegiance, and Alex
wouldn't stand for the Pledge of Allegiance, and the school
called me and told me he wouldn't stand up. They said that he
had to stand; he didn't have to say the Pledge of Allegiance,
but he had to stand. Alex refused to stand, and I had to go
in and fight for my son's right not to stand during the Pledge
of Allegiance. If we were truly a free society, it should be our
decision whether we stand or not. However, we won that battle.

It's funny; you don't realize how much of an advocate you
have to be. I just did what I thought any parent would do.
People were telling me that I was such an advocate—that
I'd changed things in the school, or I was there, on top of it.
Sometimes I think I didn't do anywhere near enough. I did all
that I could and all that I thought was right. And sometimes,
I think about the things I did that were wrong. We all make
mistakes. I forced Alex to do stuff that was wrong. Or maybe
it wasn't wrong; it was just testing the waters.

My Mother

A contribution by Alex's
mother, Allyson

Writing about my son Alex is a very difficult thing for me to do without getting on an emotional roller coaster, filled with joy, hope, sadness, and fear.

My pregnancy with Alex was a wonderful experience for Alex's father and myself. After a poor experience during the birth of our first child, we chose a home birth for Alex. Alex came into this world on a Sunday morning, straight into our arms. All fingers and toes were there, and there was no hint of anything different about him.

As Alex settled into the world, he was very attached to being held by his father or myself, and he was constantly nursing. At about 8 weeks, when I had to return to work, Alex was still unwilling to be put down for even a few moments. I remember hanging a jump swing, made for much older babies, from the doorjamb in the kitchen, and putting Alex inside and surrounding him with towels and baby blankets to support his head. The slight bounce finally gave our arms a rest. Alex was a fixture in the bounce swing for the first 8 months of his life. You could always find him there, jumping, bouncing, and laughing.

As Alex grew, he showed great patience for a child and was willing to play with his blocks, Brio trains, and Legos for hours on end, happily, by himself. He did not want solid foods for a very long time and drank rice milk from a bottle until he bit the last of the nipples off and was told there were no more bottles left in the world. Alex was about 2 at the time, and he showed great perseverance and frustration when things did not go his way. We thought Alex just needed a little more discipline and had to learn what NO meant. But Alex, unlike our other children, did not seem to take well to any sort of change. A change in schedule would upset him. The absence of his favorite food choice (peanut butter and jelly), which was the only food he ate for a year or two, would also disturb him. His favorite shirt not being clean, or the smallest of changes, would set Alex off into sobs that cut right through to your heart. These were not the cries of an insolent child, but the cries of real, internal pain, for which his father and I were at a loss.

I personally did not have any idea how to parent a child like Alex. I gave in to his every whim to avoid the tantrums and tears. Should I have disciplined him more? I fed him the only foods he wanted, peanut butter and jelly or Ellio's frozen pizza, for years. Should I have forced a more healthful diet? Our home was hectic with four children, and I was an only child. The experience of a noisy family was new to me, and I did not know how to cope. I went to work full time, and we were lucky to be able to afford a nanny. Beth stayed with us for a number of years, and I do not know what we would have done without her.

Jim, Alex's father, worked long hours and weekends, building up a business to support the family. I was not emotionally equipped to handle four little children. Years later, I received a diagnosis of depression, and I wish I had gotten a diagnosis and sought treatment years earlier. Would that have helped with my parenting skills? Would it have made a difference for Alex if I had been more patient? My children knew I loved them, I just think I was not as involved as I should have been as Alex's mom.

Alex attended kindergarten for 2 years and was encouraged to participate with the other children, but he frequently had "meltdowns." His early school years were very hard for

Alex. However, the presence of Mrs Anderson as his special-education teacher, starting in kindergarten, became his safety zone. Alex worked with Mrs Anderson for his entire school career, and I believe it was because of her unwavering patience with Alex that he made it through school. Since the school was very small, Alex had the same 15-20 kids in every grade, from kindergarten through high school. These kids befriended Alex, showed him kindness and understanding, and helped Alex with his social skills. They welcomed Alex into their activities, even though he seldom joined in, and they invited him to parties that he often attended. The kids made concessions for Alex when they knew a certain behavior or noise bothered him, and they protected him from those who would mock or bully. They were truly a special set of kids.

The divorce between me and Alex's father certainly created a downward spiral for Alex when he was 11 years old. In the beginning, Alex felt that he should not exist if his parents no longer loved each other. And no matter how hard his father and I tried to explain to him that this was not the case, Alex was distraught. At this time, we had Alex tested, and he received a diagnosis of Asperger's syndrome. This did not come as a shock to his father or me, nor did it really change anything in Alex's world. It allowed him to get more services at the school and to be declared disabled, to help him later in life, but Alex was already getting one-on-one help at school. His father and I took him to a therapist for a while, and his father searched for some schools that might work better for Alex, but nothing seemed better then what he had already.

His father and I lived close to each other, and we split the week up. It took Alex a long time to adjust to going back and forth, but it was always clear that Alex was much more comfortable at his dad's home. Clearly, his father had much more patience than I did, and, admittedly, I did not handle the divorce well. So, for Alex, his father's house probably felt less stressful.

I tried building a garage with a mini-apartment above it for Alex at my home, because he felt that my house was too small. But in the end, Alex didn't find much comfort there, either. At this time, Alex and his younger sister Katie were not getting along. Katie had no patience with Alex, and she had her own feelings of not being loved as much as Alex, as well as other typical middle-child feelings. I had just recently remarried, and Alex had a very good relationship with his stepfather. I decided that I would move to Maine with my new husband and Katie to start a new life as an innkeeper and chef, a dream I had always had. Alex's dad was still in the process of looking for schools for Alex, and we thought the distance from Katie would be helpful in developing her own sense of self. So when Alex was 15, I moved to Maine. I had plans for Alex to come and visit often, but in hindsight, I should have known better; change never works for Alex.

Since my move, however, I have had some of my closest moments with Alex. He spent a week with us the second Christmas we were in Maine. We spent the week trimming the tree, baking, and doing traditional Christmas things, and Alex told me he had the best Christmas since the divorce. It was quiet and calm—just how he liked it. The year after that, I developed an autoimmune disorder. It has kept me in and out of a wheelchair and too weak to do too much in the way of activities. Alex has spent time with me in the past few years, just watching and critiquing movies with me, sharing his hopes and dreams, and telling me he doesn't blame me for any of the choices I made.

The times I spend now with Alex are amazing; he has no "speed bump" between his brain and his mouth, and he feels free to tell me EVERYTHING he may think about. I certainly get more information than most mothers do from their sons. He tells me all his dreams, the realistic and the not so realistic.

I want the world to see Alex in all the wonderful ways that those who know and love Alex do. He is a caring, loving, and genuine human being, who just wants love and happiness in his life.

One last note—Alex is truly empathetic, a trait we were told would be impossible for someone like Alex to have. This always saddened me, because how can you go through life without having any understanding or empathy for others? But Alex is full of empathy, and the first time I saw it was when he was 7 years old, and we took a family vacation to Punta Cana, to an all-inclusive resort.

Alex was not particularly happy with the resort. He did not care for how any of the food tasted, and the soda fountain didn't have Dr Pepper; the soft ice cream was no good. We did our best to have a good vacation, but for me, it had a black cloud over it because Alex was not enjoying himself. I just wanted him to have a good time. Anyway, on the second to last day of the trip, we took a tour to go see something outside of the resort. We drove through desert land, where there was not much to see, other than a few goats, people walking, and scattered huts. The van stopped for a moment in front of a concrete hut with three walls, and the front was covered by a curtain. A goat was outside, and a small family was gathered.

The small children ran to the front of the bus, begging for candy. Alex watched the children and the family, and then the van began to move. "What was that building?" he asked the driver. "That is their house," he said. "For ALL of them?" Alex asked, and the driver explained to Alex that the family was very poor, so about six to eight people would live together like that. He told Alex they brought in water, and that the goat gave them milk. Alex asked about their car, and the driver explained that they had none. Alex was quiet for the rest of the day.

When we got back home, at school, he was asked to write about his vacation. Alex wrote about the family in the hut, with no clean clothes, no car, and no money. Alex wrote that if everyone on Shelter Island sold their cars and houses, that we could all share with the people over there. He explained that when everyone is born, they should get a "ticket" for one small car, one small house, and some money for food and clothes. If you fall in love and get married, he said, then you could get a bigger house and maybe trade your two car tickets in to get one bigger car to hold your family. Alex expounded on his ideas for weeks, trying to create a method that would make this work, until he lost interest and his brain moved on to the next great project to make the world a better place.

Alex asked me one day why I had an autism sticker on the back of my car. I told him that when his stepfather and I got married, we gave one to everyone who came to the wedding, and we made a donation on behalf of him. He asked me what "Autism Awareness" did, and I told them they developed programs for children like him and were also looking for the cause of and cure for autism and Asperger's syndrome. He said to me, "I don't want them to cure Asperger's." I asked him why, and he said, "Because that's what makes me, and I like me." I hugged him tight and told him I loved him just the way he is, too.

My Stepmother

A contribution by Alex's
stepmother, Kate

I first met Alex when he was 10 years old; he was a very cute, big blue-eyed boy. I found him to be sweet and thoughtful. He is definitely the most reserved of his three siblings. When he talks, he really likes to talk. The conversation is usually one-sided, but he's always exuberant and passionate about what he discusses.

One of the first times I noticed his unease in social settings was when he came over to my parents' house in Shelter Island for a barbeque. His sisters and brother blended in well with my nieces. Alex stood out in the crowd. I could see he was having a hard time taking in all these new faces. By that I mean he would walk in a circle constantly. Not a big circle—it was like he was marking his space. He would talk as he walked. He looked down at the floor and made no eye contact. It was curious. I knew he was struggling to take it all in. For the most part, I knew he required extra-special care, and that's how I handled Alex.

Did it take a long time to understand Alex? Sometimes. The overstimulation of his senses is hard to understand. He's walked on his tiptoes forever. Pressing his feet on the floor bothers him. He can't stand the feeling of writing with a pencil; therefore, he never uses a pencil.

Alex's diet has gotten better, and he now includes a few veggies and fruit. But for a long time, he sustained on hot dogs and pasta with Parmesan cheese. If I picked up the wrong brand of hot dog rolls, for example, Alex would not eat them.

Understanding him on an emotional level is not that big of a deal. I see him as a gentle, kind, innocent, blatantly honest human being. But he is also frustrated with the outside world and feels isolated sometimes. He's really talented, and he thinks outside the box. He has his limitations, rituals, and rigid routines. If something upsets him, he can be edgy.

With Alex, I try to be compassionate and patient. I let him be who he is. I don't try to change him. Instead, I listen to what he says and try to understand and encourage him. I try to think of a situation where I am uncomfortable. I can't stand driving across high bridges. I imagine that when Alex is having "a moment," it must be similar to my fear of bridges.

Alex is 21 now, and he's progressed amazingly in the last 10 years. He's so much more at ease in dealing with people. He likes his hugs now. He was a lot more withdrawn in the past when it came to human contact.

I think with Alex, there are endless possibilities. He is a terrific speaker. He has no fear of talking to the public. He's very focused on creating. He's now writing a book, and he researches his material meticulously. It's really important for Alex to have goals.

There are many stories. One that stands out is last Christmas. We all experience some stress during the holidays. But stress took on a whole new meaning on Christmas day. Alex, as always, turns his computer on first thing in the morning. Well, that morning, the computer wasn't responding. Alex went into a slight panic, wondering what was up. He's very good at fixing computer glitches. When it became apparent that he couldn't fix the problem, he came upstairs to the kitchen to find his father and started weeping. He implored his father to call Mike, the computer expert, to come over and fix it. Mike was understandably away for the holidays. Alex's anxiety became a full-blown panic attack.

The kids and I watched in silence as Jim, his father, calmed him down. Jim is the only one who has the ability to do that. Alex was on edge all day. He didn't want to interact with anyone and was on the verge of tears.

The next day, Mike discovered that Alex's computer hard drive was fried, and it had basically crashed. We were all affected that Christmas day by the intensity of grief that Alex experienced. We had 25 family members over for dinner, and in the back of my mind, I couldn't help thinking, is Alex going to be okay?

28

My Stepfather

A contribution by Alex's stepfather, Don

I have known Alex for almost 8 years. In that time, Alex has shown an extreme improvement in his ability to interact with others. When I first met Alex, he would spend most of his time with me reciting (verbatim) episodes of various cartoons or discussing some of his ideas. Since I am a person who likes cartoons, this certainly has helped him.

At the time, I would sit, listen, and share what interested Alex, without attempting to direct the topic or steer our relationship in any way, allowing him to stay in his comfort zone. In hindsight, I think this is one of the reasons we have such a good relationship.

My advice to other parents would be to remember that when interacting with someone like Alex, you are entering his world and his perception of it. The best thing you can do is to enjoy your time in his world and not try and change him or push him into exiting his world.

My Teacher

A contribution by Alex's resource room teacher, Mrs Anderson

I first met Alex when I became his resource room teacher when he began first grade. He was a small, blond-haired, blue-eyed boy with a very distinctive gaze. I would come get him off the playground each day, where he would be walking in a large circle. (For many years, there remained a circular path in the grass where Alex walked during recess.) I always asked him what he had been thinking about, and this would get him started. He would tell me as we walked back to my classroom, and he would be so full of his thoughts that it would be hard to get him to pause long enough for me to get a word in about what we were going to do that day.

Alex did not have difficulty with math, but he struggled with reading. In second grade, Alex was still struggling with the letters of the alphabet and their sounds. Then one day in November, he suddenly understood that there was a pattern and rules to the process of decoding. At that time, we were using decoding keys and a linguistic reader. We were doing a page in a workbook called "Explode the Code," and we were working with the "at" key. He suddenly saw that "at" stayed the same but that when a new letter was put in front of it, that sound was added, and a new word was made..."cat," "mat," "hat," and so on. I remember Alex laboriously trying each letter out, blending its sound with "at." He was excited by the fact that he had found the "key to the lock," but he was not nearly as thrilled as I was. After that, Alex began to learn basic decoding skills, and some of his frustration with school decreased.

Alex always seemed to process things as pictures rather than words. He did not know the names of his classmates, but he could describe them in great detail. As people became meaningful in his life, he eventually learned their names.

However, even as a senior, he could not name all of his class-mates, even though he had been with some of them for his entire school career.

Alex's visual-motor skills were amazing. When he drew something, he always used black pen. He would start with some tiny detail, and an entire image would grow from it. Sometimes, he drew these incredibly detailed "inventions;" other times, he drew a favorite cartoon character. He was able to capture the essence of a character or a person with simple lines. Although Alex loved the computer and all the things he could do with it, I was saddened by the fact that his other drawings stopped as he increasingly embraced technology.

I was always amazed at Alex's auditory memory, as well. He could repeat an entire episode of SpongeBob, verbatim, or pick up an interrupted conversation exactly where he had left off, mid-sentence, even if considerable time had elapsed. If the topic was something he was interested in, he remembered every detail.

Seventh through ninth grades are normally stressful years for most students, and they were particularly difficult years for Alex. It was during this time that we developed our ritual of having a cup of tea and a conversation, and sometimes watching a video clip of a show or something else he enjoyed watching to help him calm down and give him time to work through the stress, so we could eventually get through what-ever had to be done. Alex spent more time in the resource room, and he refused to do any schoolwork at home. He stayed after school every day to do his work. It was not always easy to balance the educational mandates of public school with the practical and social skills necessary for life after high school and Alex's wish to avoid things that caused him stress.

I remained Alex's resource room teacher throughout his school years. Once or twice, scheduling conflicts placed him with another teacher, but this did not seem to work and did not last. Having one consistent person in school seemed to be best for Alex. By the time he was in middle school, we had developed a trust that made it possible to get through the stressful parts of his day. At the end of seventh grade, Alex gave me a framed picture he had done, which said, "To Mrs Anderson, my only adult friend. From Alex Olinkiewicz." To know that I had Alex's trust meant a great deal to me.

The most difficult thing to deal with when Alex was in high school was his need to eliminate stress from his life, as well as his belief that he shouldn't have to deal with it. We talked often of my fear for him that his world would become smaller and smaller if he let the thought of stress limit him— if he did not learn to deal with some stress. No life is stress free, and we all have to find some way to handle it, not just avoid it.

As with all students, there is no one way or style of teaching that works with everyone. It depends on the individual, the specific situation, the needs, and the personalities involved. In our particular case, Alex's success in school was probably strongly connected to the consistency of having one person as a resource room teacher throughout his school years and the relationship that developed as a result.

My Book's Collaborator

A contribution by Dr O'Connell

During the time of my working with Alex over a period of 2 years, I have come to know him very well.

Alex is a very pleasant person. He has a sense of humor and is quite intelligent. He has a mind of his own and is very incisive in his thinking. He has challenged me constantly and held firm that *In My Mind* is his book, and it's to be done the way he wants it. And he is right practically all of the time in what he requires.

As is obvious from reading his book, he has an analytical mind. He can explain in graphic detail the experiences he relates. In addition to that, he has a great sense of metaphor in how he describes through his graphics various aspects of his Asperger's syndrome. This quality has enabled him to articulate profound insights as to the nature of his disorder.

When someone is handicapped, as Alex is with his Asperger's, he could easily become egocentric, but this isn't the case with Alex. He does have feelings for other people and can make accommodations. There is a genuine part of him that wants to please. When he's in uncomfortable situations he may become ornery, but this really is a defense mechanism to deal with his inner struggles.

One of the things I had to watch out for is laying too many requirements on his shoulders. Alex cannot deal with overload and begins to have anxiety if he has to deal with many chores at once. He has difficulty prioritizing his problems or tasks and consequently begins to obsess about them, which increases his anxiety. The experience of writing his book in its peculiar development was a good lesson in delayed satisfaction, as well as being patient with people with whom he had to work. Not everyone works at the same pace, and putting together a book like this is complicated and time consuming. Throughout the process, Alex has learned patience and has come to an understanding that a book like his and the life of someone with Asperger's are not all that simple.

In working with Alex, I have found one of his defense mechanisms is his tendency to pass on some of his chores to other people or to bypass a request by ignoring it. In the course of collaborating with him in this book, I would make reference to material I had previously sent him. Alex would, on occasion, ask me to send the material again, rather than look it up himself. He is a computer whiz, and the task was easily within his realm. Alex should examine other areas where he may tend to use this mechanism to avoid more personal involvement or extra work. This is important for developing his own sense of independence. Alex should ask himself, "Am I capable of doing this? Am I requesting someone else to do a task that I am completely capable of doing?"

I have found some areas of seeming contradiction. Alex says he can't read long paragraphs. Yet, when it came to his book, he managed to do so. Alex can't stand Thanksgiving because of all the noise and confusion, yet he loves Christmas, with all its social gatherings. It may be because at Christmas, there is so much joy involved, he can block out some of those things he finds difficult ordinarily. It is my hope that Alex reads this and grows by my observations.

Alex is a very honest person, and he prides himself on his integrity. There were times when he was under a great deal of pressure and could not get involved in the project over a long period of time. There were times when material in the book was extensive, and work would not be done. Alex has to examine these times and consider if there were some times of less pressure when he could have done a little more work. Alex has to learn to see those glimpses of light shining through those areas of overload when he can achieve, even if it is a small amount, rather than seeing the picture as a totally unattainable goal. Realizing how difficult this can be for Alex, I feel it is worth mentioning here so that by taking small steps, he will become more capable of achieving his life's dreams.

During the course of writing this book, I have seen a higher degree of maturation taking place. As Alex comments, he lives in two worlds. The difficulty here is that Alex does not see the world of our reality as totally as he should. He sees things mostly from his perspective, which, by the nature of his mindset, is limited. What has transpired through frequent conversations and disagreements is that he has come to have a broader outlook on certain issues and circumstances.

Over the past 2 years, I have seen real growth in Alex as a public speaker. With the success of his YouTube video, he has gained much confidence. This has been reinforced by the wonderful reviews given at his presentations. This is quite an achievement for anyone, let alone a young man with Asperger's syndrome.

An outcome of this book will not be the number of sales it achieves. It will not be the fact that Alex has written a book that will be helpful to people. Rather, it is the joy and satisfaction that Alex has had in anticipation of the publishing of his book. To see this gives great joy to all who have worked with Alex to help produce the book. This alone has been worth the effort.

Finally, by going through the whole process of compiling this book, Alex must realize that he has achieved what so few people are capable of doing ... writing his own book. This

achievement will hopefully give him the internal impetus to tackle his other dreams with determination and courage.

My Talk with a Parent Whose Son Has Asperger's Syndrome

Alex, today we are with a parent (Eileen) who would like to hear your comments on some of your Asperger's issues.

EILEEN: We are in a large public school system, and my son has Asperger's, and the system doesn't give very good service.

In fact, my son was kicked out of the public school. They were unwilling to work with or help him, and the school had no placement for him whatsoever. People are shocked to hear this, but it's the truth. I had to find a private school for my son, and pay for it, and then try to have the board of education reimburse me. So I had to hire an attorney, and he had to fight with them to get reimbursed for this, because my child is entitled to an education. And I feel that a lot of school systems outside of the city help children like my son. In the city, they just don't want to help us; they just push us of off somewhere else.

They tell us to go somewhere else, to go find it ourselves, to help ourselves. And I toured a lot of schools in the city. Some of the schools in the public school system are warehousing these kids. They don't have special-education teachers in them, when they're supposed to. They have padded rooms. I walked into a classroom where the teachers were screaming at a little 5-year-old boy, because he couldn't speak, and he was sitting there crying. Every time I came out of these tours, I was shaking. It was just unbelievable. Everybody thinks a large city would be so great for this, but it's been very hard for us.

ALEX: I'd have to agree with that. For any school that's supposed to have special education, that's not the way that they are supposed to teach or help a kid with a disorder. Doing things like yelling at a child or screaming doesn't really help him learn. He just ends up breaking down, and then he doesn't really pay attention to what's going on. I had an advantage of being at the school that I was in, which is on the island. It had its advantages. Even though you're having a hard time finding a school for your child, at least when you find it, it will be large and have of a lot of kids. The odds are good that your son is going to find another kid that is just like him—someone he can relate to.

The latest statistic is that one person in 88 receives a diagnosis of Asperger's syndrome or autism. In my school, there were about 200 students in the whole school, from preschool all the way up to high school. And you want to know how many people in that school had a form of autism or Asperger's when I went? Just one, and that was me. This has changed. *When I was in that school, there were times when I tried to hang out with friends, but I was very lonely.* There were teachers like Mrs Anderson, and she was a big help to me. If not for her, I would have felt extremely lonely there.

RICHARD: Did you make any friends?

ALEX: I feel like I did, but I'm not really sure. Even though I saw one or two of them around at times, there were never moments when I hung out with them. I did try, but I always felt like an outcast. I'd try to get in a conversation, and in the end, they never really talked about the same topics that I did. Or when I tried to jump into their conversations, their conversations would just end there.

EILEEN: That's because you seem to communicate really well, whereas my son has a language delay. So I'm wondering what he's feeling, because he can't tell me. It's not that he can't express himself. I have been able to understand him perfectly fine, even though he has a delay. I just understand that he doesn't show any sign of disappointment toward his lack of social contact. He shows a lot of happiness, and he smiles, which is good. I think the real worry is when he gets older; he will slowly understand more things about life. That's what I'm concerned about. I was hoping you could help me with that. That's the unknown. I know what we've gone through, but I'm worried about other kids—his being teased. I'm worried about how he feels about himself. How do I explain to his little 5-year-old brother, Harry, when he asks why his brother does the things he does? And I have to say, "Well, we're all a little different. I do things kind of strange, and he's really good at certain things, and you're really good at certain things." And I just don't know what to say to him when he asks, "Why does David do the things he does?"

ALEX: That's always one of the things that concerns a lot of parents—the hardest thing about your child having a disorder is wondering when it's proper to let your kids know about it. When your kid asks where babies come from, you don't start by telling him the actual details. You can start by telling him it's the stork, or you can tell him that you're going to have to wait until he gets older to tell him. But unfortunately, we're not learning about where babies come from here. You can't tell your sons that you'll explain it when they're older. The problem is there's never really a good time to tell your children about a disorder. There isn't a specific age. Don't wait until they're older. I know some people who spend their whole lives—until they're in their forties—questioning themselves, wondering what is wrong with them, until they find out what it is. When a kid has a problem and he doesn't know what it is—try telling him then. One time when I was a preteen, before I knew I had Asperger's syndrome, there was a person in my class who came up to me and asked me, "Why do you get all this special treatment? Why do you get all this happy stuff?" And it made me feel upset because my life is not that great. But I do get this special treatment.

EILEEN: Was he jealous?

ALEX: Well, I think he was jealous, because he didn't know about my disorder. And that's ultimately the problem. Your kid is going to have special treatment, as well, so he needs to learn what works for his mind, but when everybody sees it, they'll think that he's the "special one." He's the "teacher's pet" or something like that, and that could lead to teasing your son. When a kid gets nice treatment from the teacher, he gets teased because the other kids are jealous.

EILEEN: My son David is in a school where all the kids are like him. There are 10 kids in his class, all boys, because obviously it seems to affect more boys than girls. He only has 10 kids in the class and two teachers. So he doesn't get that experience where kids are going to say, "Oh you're getting special attention." That's the good thing at this time of his life, because he's with kids who are like him, and they can relate to him. Everybody at the school understands what we're going through. Before that, it was very lonely for him, and very lonely for me, too. I felt very lonely for him—David knew how lonely it was for us.

We're very fortunate we've found this school, but this is his fourth school, and he's only 7. So it's been a lot of bouncing around to get to the right place. So we're lucky. We're very, very lucky. And everyone there knows how to help him—the teachers are all educated in the field, so they're really good. They don't care what they have to do; he can sit on a bouncy seat and have sensory breaks. They do everything they can to get him to learn, to read, to write, to learn. It's amazing.

ALEX: I understand, again, your main problem and concern is when he has to go out of that class and into a different class. And you hope someday he can be in a regular school.

EILEEN: That's what our hope is.

ALEX: Well, hopefully with my book, it will change a lot of people's views on the issues we have been speaking about.

EILEEN: My son David has a lot of stims, like talking like a dog, or running around a certain way, or patting his cheeks when he's excited. Did you have any stims, and do you feel like they diminish over time?

ALEX: There are few reasons why he acts the way he does and why I do things like that. You have to remember that when it comes to us, we have two different worlds that we live in. There's the world we create, and there's the real world.

I feel like I'm always in another world. Right now, it's just because I'm more mature and I'm grown that I know how to control it, but when I'm by myself sometimes, if I listen to music, you might see me jump around, pretending I'm in the shoes of one of the characters from my stories. When I'm watching some review of a movie or something of interest, I end up discussing my views to an audience of no one. I literally talk to myself like I'm making a commentary video for YouTube or something similar.

That's my own world. The thing is, everyone has their own world to begin with, when they're a child. You know how kids always pretend when they're young—they have tea parties or war games? Those are our other worlds that we've created. When we get older, we abandon those worlds. However, people like me, we still have them, and we never abandon them. Our own world stays with us for the rest of our lives. The world David is in is his sanctuary. We have trouble when it comes to being in the real world because of how certain things feel, sound, and behave. However, when we're in our own world, we black out some of those problems. What he is doing now is using his world to avoid all the issues and problems going on around him.

EILEEN: A lot of times he makes noises—I notice this when he's bored, especially when he's bored. He'll run around, back and forth, going "woowoowooowooo," like a siren. He only does this when he's bored, and I don't understand.

ALEX: I can explain this. It's something that I do too. I don't run around, but I pace a lot, and I enter my world again. This is the same thing that happens to him if he's excited. If he's excited, he does the pat on the cheek, or he tugs at his hair. If he's bored, he runs around in circles and goes "woooooooo." What happens if he's in a stressful moment? How does he deal with that?

EILEEN: He kind of quivers up and bangs his head a bit. When we witness any form of this, it comes from a certain things that upset him or something that makes him happy. He behaves very differently.

ALEX: When I am in a room that is completely uncomfortable to me, my mind will overthink things. Like the feeling in my hand—is it going to stop? Is time moving slower? Is time going faster? How long do I have to be in this room? When do

I get to leave? It's like an anxiety attack. Our minds overthink things so much. What we're doing is distracting part of our minds with another activity. When he's bored, you know how your mind feels when you're bored? It just feels empty? He's keeping his mind active by running around with his voice and his body. He's moving his body and using his voice to make his mind active. When he's excited, he's patting his cheeks and feeling the pressure of his hand against his cheeks, trying to distract him from all the excitement that makes him feel stressed out! If he experiences the stress, it feels to him like he's going to lose it.

Because if you think about it, he's not going crazy or worrying about things; he's just sitting there patting his cheeks a bit. Or when he's sad, he does that—beating his head. *What he's trying to do is beat out the sad and make it go away.* It's a distraction mechanism that we use to distract part of our mind.

EILEEN: I didn't realize that, because this is the one thing we've been trying to have David overcome as much as possible, and have him cope with stress via traditional methods. It's basically coping skills, I guess. Could you tell us how you have grown out of some of these things?

ALEX: There are things I do when I'm nervous. Sometimes when I'm very uncomfortable, my legs twitch, my hands tap constantly. My mind races. I discovered when I was in the Department of Motor Vehicles with a friend that patting my hand was less obvious to the public and helpful to me. Even still, I was very uncomfortable in my chair; I needed to keep my eyes closed because of the environment. The lights...the crowds...I was trying to do my typical techniques, like tapping my fingers on my knee, and I couldn't find the right, comfortable position. So in the end, I settled on this one move that I think I may use for the tranquility of my mind, which was patting on my left hand.

A lot of people who are autistic, who have a hard time when their environment isn't right, end up doing things such as wiggling their fingers and swirling their hands around. I consider it to be like the hypnosis wheel. They're hypnotizing their minds with the hypnotize wheel, or just putting a little bit of pressure on a part of their body, because the brain is constantly at it. But, I notice that these things can change. David is constantly changing and evolving. It's always the case when people get older. Their methods change in different ways.

EILEEN: I tell David, "In your mind, imagine you are squeezing your hands against your head, and squeeze them tight!"

ALEX: And squeezing his hands tight is basically the same thing. It's a mind distraction. I'm actually surprised that not a lot of people realize that's why we do =these kinds of things. It's a distraction for when our minds are very active. We mostly try these methods to be distracted, so we don't go haywire.

EILEEN: That's good to know. I didn't know that. I was trying to understand that about him, and how to stop him, and there's no way of stopping him. I guess it's just redirecting his habits when feasible.

ALEX: Don't try to stop it. If it wasn't for that habit, he could probably end up breaking down. If you prevent him from doing something that helps distract his mind, he'll become upset. If I sit completely still and do nothing, it's going to cause my body to get so irritated. But doing something simple like he does, which might be a little annoying to some people, because it looks odd, feels better. You've got to know that this is his way of relaxing. Isn't his way of relaxing amazing? It is a form of stimming.*

RICHARD: Alex, you spoke of not trying to change stimming, which is not harming children. I regard this as one of your personal views and may not be in agreement with some Asperger's specialists.

ALEX: This may be the case, but some form of relief should be allowed for the child, perhaps a modified type of stimming. If a change is attempted, from my point of view, it should be done gradually and positively. Quitting "cold turkey" never worked with me, and I have changed some of my stimming to some other type of relief. I still need a distraction when my mind is overloaded or panicking.

RICHARD: In chapter 7 on "awkward and uncoordinated movements," you mentioned that you picked up the habit of sitting Indian style before kindergarten. Do you think if you were encouraged back then to change and were not allowed to make this a comforting position that today you would not have this habit?

---

* According to "Autism Speak," stimming is basically the actions and behaviors used to help a person on the autism spectrum calm the nervous system. Self-stimming is a way to "scratch" a "neurological itch." Some common forms include rocking, flapping, rolling, spinning, bouncing, head-banging on a pillow to get to sleep, jumping on a trampoline, swinging on a hammock, feeling tactile elements or textured materials, kicking, tapping feet or fingers, and clapping hands.

ALEX: That is hard to say, but I know today that it would be very, very hard to change. It is part of my lifestyle. I probably adopted this sitting position because it helped to ease the discomfort I have from standing for a long period of time. My feet have a strange feeling when I have to sit differently, and I become very distracted.

EILEEN: Alex, how do you view stimming with regard to habits other "normal" people have?

ALEX: So many people in this world do odd things to relax, but it's just a degree of how much. You're describing what a lot of people feel in many ways. That's basically the point, it's just that—there's a spectrum, and "the main perspective" is where most people are, and we're just slightly more out of it than they are. Here's what you should know. When it comes to all the problems you might come across with your son, you should never blame his disorder. Why? Because it is not really him that is the problem. It's the community—it is their problem. You have to remember, the average person fits the accepted norm. But others haven't really made accommodations for us to fit in.

Others are not accepting of diversity. That's what my problem is. Because people like me look fine, but our minds and our behaviors work differently, and other people can't "see" it, they don't think there is something they need to adjust for us. I agree with you 100 percent. Society hasn't accepted David and me. Have you ever met someone, and you think they're rude, they don't say hello to you? I say to myself, there's more to their being rude. Maybe they have some social issues. Why can't we see that? If you open your mind, you might see that they're not rude; they may just not be able to socialize. And I give people a bigger break than I ever did before, because, it's easy to just say they're rude and not look deeper.

Whenever I'm on the phone with someone, like a service, I always like to start by letting them know I have a disorder. That way, they're aware that if something I say is wrong, or there's something I don't understand, then they can understand me better. They will understand that I have a disorder.

EILEEN: How do you say that when you're talking to those people?

ALEX: Oh I just say, "Before we begin, I want you to know that I have a diagnosis of Asperger's syndrome, and there are some things I don't understand. I might ask you to slow down." And they say, "That's fine, I understand, sir." And then they're very nice and helpful. It definitely makes a difference.

I feel that when a person walks into a building, most people do not see the autistic person in the right way. When they see someone in a wheelchair or someone who is blind, people know that that person needs some support.

EILEEN: That's a really great point. I never thought of that.

ALEX: That's how everyone views each other when they first see each other. They instantly think that if that person looks normal, he or she is in their own "spectrum." Basically, you have to let other people know about your limitations, because if you don't, they'll think you're in their "zone." Unless you let them know, somehow you just seem so strange. Let them know that you're not some crazy guy—just a guy who's out of their spectrum.

EILEEN: How would you advise a parent concerning her other children, when it comes to having a sibling with Asperger's?

When should siblings know that one of their siblings has this kind of disability, and what's the best way of doing that?

ALEX: This is the tough part. It's always hard to figure out when it is the proper time to tell your kids. On one hand, it seems all right to just wait until they're older. But on the other hand, if they don't know, then they won't know why most people misjudge their brother. And they will have a harder time understanding why other people act differently around their brother.

If a kid goes into school, and the kid is being specially treated and he doesn't know the reason why, and everyone else doesn't know why, he and they will think he's just like everyone else. You have to slowly and surely educate everyone. It's something you have to give bit by bit. It's the right way, because he is autistic and he doesn't understand yet what a disorder is, and he just needs to know that he has some gifts that are different from other kids. This is how my parents told me when I was young.

I could relate how I learned that I had autism. I was taken to a doctor I had never been with before. And I was given these weird little tests to do. I could play with toys or tell a story from a book with no words, just pictures, and then I was asked a few questions. And, later, my parents were informed about my diagnosis. Later, they talked with me about how I act. I think this is the way you should start off—with a simple explanation. You don't tell the child his actual diagnosis. One thing is for sure—don't say "disorder." There are still many views on what a disorder is. There are disorders that actually have nothing good about them, but then there are disorders that have a gift to them.

In general, Asperger's is misunderstood, because people view the bad parts of that disorder but not the good parts. For me, Asperger's has some good parts. Did you ever hear the term, neurodiversity?

EILEEN: No, I don't think so.

ALEX: Okay, there's a group of people who believe that instead of calling Asperger's a disorder, it should be referred to as a form of neurodiversity. It's a different way of looking at it, and they want people to embrace it. I think right now, the reason that I'm sticking with the word "disorder" is because Asperger's is considered a disorder. People understand that way now. Secondly, that other phrase, that's not really a word I can remember saying.

So you have regular, typical development versus neurodiversity. I read an article on it, and it's one of the best articles I've read on this kind of terminology.

At first, what you say to your kids should be clear, simple, and understandable at the child's level.

EILEEN: How old were you when your parents first told you?

ALEX: I was 6. But they didn't tell me I was autistic at first. What they told me probably works best for now; you might want to do it much more slowly. Maybe my parents should have told me a lot sooner than that, but it's not as bad as it was. Right now, you can say, "Your mind works differently than others." That's the simplest way I can think of. That is really the case. His mind works way different than almost everyone else.

EILEEN: He's all the things you mentioned. And I tell him all these things because I want him to have confidence, and it's true. I'm not embellishing. He's so smart, he's so creative, he's a good thinker, and he's a little genius. He is going to do great things in this world. I am fully convinced. It's unbelievable. He can ask you, "When's your birthday?" and you'll say, "May 8th," and he'll say, "That was a Friday." And you'll go look it up on your smart phone, and, sure enough—it was that day! He's got a photographic memory of these things. I was waiting for his little gift to come out for many years. And finally, he's showing it. He can remember anything. I can go to an apartment in the city; I ask him, "What floor is it on?" He'll say, "7C," and he just knows it. It's unbelievable. His genius is unbelievable.

What's puzzling me now is, how fast should you educate your child to be aware of his diversity? It seems like you should do it gradually.

ALEX: Well, part of my development was, as I got older, I got wiser. I found other solutions to help me cope. When I was a kid, and I didn't know about my disorder, the only thing I got was that my mind worked differently. Other times, I was told that I was "special."

EILEEN: Did you feel different?

ALEX: Well, I seemed to be an outcast to a lot of people. And when I had problems, people would question me or argue with me. When I was a kid, I couldn't give them a proper explanation.

EILEEN: Did you feel happy?

ALEX: A lot of times I was happy, but then there were other times I was sad. People did not understand me. The times where I was in my own world, I was happy. The times I was around people, I wasn't as happy, because I wasn't understood.

EILEEN: Did your parents understand you?

ALEX: Oh yeah. My parents pretty much understood me, and they mostly accepted my choices and thoughts, and that was good. They learned more and more how to deal with me as I grew up.

EILEEN: How did you cope?

ALEX: When I was young and I behaved differently, there were moments I felt that I shouldn't do strange things. You know how some parents have trouble with their kids when they go into a grocery store, and their kids are misbehaving, and all the parents and people are staring at them, and the kids don't notice, but you do? And if you were that kid, you would realize you should stop doing that behavior, so you are not noticed. I was like that. I was in that position where I was aware of what people thought of me—I wasn't aware that it was because of my disorder, I just thought that everyone thought I was a weirdo or something. So, I never tried to do certain things that I may have wanted to do. I was born more like a mature person; I grow much faster than other people.

Making my YouTube video really me with one thing. This is me. I should not let anyone get in the way of who I am.

Sometimes, if I am in the supermarket, especially at this age, there are times where I behave a bit childish. I walk silly, I move crazy, and I'm just trying to be in my world. And if everyone stares at me, I just understand that they don't understand. There's nothing wrong with me—they don't understand me, and that's it. Even though I usually seem to behave like the average person, I am still far away from the norm. I am nowhere near that average point.

EILEEN: Did you have any motor-skill issues, like with writing? Did you need a lot of occupational therapy or any other type of support services?

ALEX: When people look at me, the way I talk, the way I walk, the way I dress, I look like a regular guy, so they see me in that perspective. You don't see me walking about the streets doing strange things.

I cannot handle being in certain bland environments, which everyone else can handle. And what I mean by bland is pale white coloring—there's no color to it. Like in the Department of Motor Vehicles. They don't bother to decorate it or give it some color; it's just a plain, blank wall. The only decorations you see are on the desks, and you never really get close enough to look at them.

EILEEN: It's interesting that you say that, because my son likes white sheets. He doesn't like too much color. He doesn't like too much color in his clothing; it has to be certain colors. He cannot wear certain colors. I am the same way, so I know how he feels.

ALEX: It's so different. Everyone is so different on the autistic spectrum. It's just like, what's your favorite color? Mine's blue. Yours is probably red or something like that. But it gets to the extreme, where I can only wear a blue shirt. There are a lot of things with me like that. You probably noticed that I'm wearing sweatpants. I cannot wear jeans. It's not the fabric, but the fact that the belt part digs in. So I have to wear anything that has elastic. Because it's a sensory feeling. And, technically, I don't prefer wearing sweatpants that much. Right now I'm okay, and usually it's okay when I go outside. To be honest, I like to wear very light clothing when I'm in a nice place. When

I'm outside in a very cold environment, it feels fine, because it makes me feel warm and cozy.

EILEEN: My son won't wear a coat in the winter. He will not wear coats even now, in the fall. Warm clothes are something he needs to wear, because he can get sick.

ALEX: He needs to find different alternatives. I don't like long-sleeved shirts. They make me want to crawl out of my skin. I always have to wear short sleeves or a sleeveless t-shirt. The only reason I don't have trouble with coats is that they're baggy. They don't get tight or wrap around your hands. It's just floating in the air. And inside the house I do take off my shirt sometimes, because the sensory feel is okay. And my mom says, "Put a shirt on." I get that sometimes from my sisters. When I go home, I change into shorts. Even during the winter, I wear shorts. And I don't wear shoes and socks when I'm in the house. Here, I'm doing something of a business nature. I'm not going to waste time taking off my shoes and putting my socks to the side. I can handle it while I'm just meeting with people, but not when I'm spending my whole day at home.

EILEEN: I get it, I totally get it. I totally understand that. That's the clothing sensory issue. I have so many sensory issues myself, that I can't begin to tell you what this kid has taught me. I know where he gets it from—me. There are a lot of things I can't wear.

Regarding playmates, we have to go to dinner with some friends on the island with some small children. My son doesn't really know how to interact with small children, but he really likes to be around kids. He likes to be there, he likes to be involved. So I spend a lot of time trying to make playdates for him, because he's still pretty little, and I am trying to facilitate as much as possible.

ALEX: I remember one time when I was a teenager; I wanted to have my own sleepovers like everyone else did. And I had my sleepover with a bunch of my friends. And guess what happened? When they were doing activities, I was not doing the activities with them. I'd tell them to go without me. And my mom would say, "Why would you even have a sleepover if you're not hanging out with your friends?" And I said, "I am hanging out with my friends!" It was a decent enough sleepover for what it was, but I don't know how well it turned out for them. My mom would say, "I'm more concerned that you're not interacting. You're perfectly happy just having them over." It's a parent's perspective. You are trying to pose what you feel onto your child. The thing is, we want to have company. Just the fact that we have company is fine, but there are things they do that I'm just not interested in.

EILEEN: So you really need to find somebody that likes to do what you like to do. And do you have any friends that like to do what you do?

ALEX: Not really. It's something that really should not be mentioned at the moment with your son. It's a growing-up lifestyle thing. And I know a few friends who are into the same things that I'm into, but that's adult stuff. That's not something you need to worry about now with your son. If he has his own beliefs and own decisions on things, make sure you respect them in every way. If parents are Christian, and their son says, "I don't believe in God," the parents go crazy about it and try to teach him that he will burn in hell. That's wrong. You should just accept his choice. The whole "following in your parents' footsteps" thing is completely wrong. Just because you're the one who brought him into the world doesn't mean he has to be like you. He is his own person. Hopefully, he'll be better for it.

I have a few friends here and there, and I remember when I was in school, there was this one foreign-exchange kid who came to my school. He was there for a while. His parents moved here because of their jobs—he used to live in France. He moved to Shelter Island with his parents, and we hung out all the time and had great experiences. We had our own secret handshakes together; we would sit at the tables together in school. We used to discuss things, and there were moments where I could tell he was a little bit of a liar. When I was a kid, I had always wanted to create my own robot. And he said, "When I was in France, I already had a robot—a fully sized robot that was able to move around and clean the house." Now that I know about robotics, I know he was lying.

EILEEN: Maybe he wanted you to like him.

ALEX: Well that's what I think, that's what I know it was. I think part of the reason I liked our relationship was that we both had something similar. I was an outcast because I had a disorder, and he was an outcast because he was a foreign student. So we related to each other in different ways. He had different views because of his culture, and I had different views because of my disorder. We related to each other. I feel like that's the reason we hung out a lot. We even had sleepovers. Unfortunately, I heard the bad news that his father decided that he preferred his old job, and they moved back to France. It was a big disappointment for me. I did have friends. And some of the friends I have now are mostly girl friends, and they're not really that bad. There's nothing wrong with that.

RICHARD: What about Liza?

ALEX: It's been a little rocky with Liza these past few days, since she has different jobs now, and her schedule has been changing so much. But we hang out as friends, we talk to each other, and we talk about personal life, so there's that, too.

RICHARD: How old is Liza?

ALEX: Liza is about 4 or 5 years older than me. She used to work for my dad at the gas station, and she volunteered to help me out, and now she doesn't work at the gas station, but she still works with me. There are still rocky moments with her and with me. When she needs to do stuff, I don't want to wait. It's a friend curse. I don't like holding up my friends.

RICHARD: Eileen, did you learn anything from talking with Alex?

EILEEN: I did, actually, about the stims. That was what was the most unknown to me. The sensory aspect I understand. I'm trying to understand the stims the best I can, and this is going to help me greatly for both of us—coping with it.

RICHARD: I hope you're encouraged to see Alex. He's grown, he's very articulate, and he's thought this out deeply.

EILEEN: It's amazing; *he's helping a lot of parents like me, who really need the support and the help.*

Addendum:
Reasons to Hope

Alex, in a recent conversation with your father, he said in the past 2½ years, you have made considerable progress in your personal life. He indicated that you should write a sequel to your completed book, recently taken over by Future Horizons, a national autism publishing company. Do you plan to do so?

Yes, and I am collecting my experiences to make the sequel.

For now, however, we will just add a small addendum to highlight your progress. What are some of the recent significant events in your life? Would you summarize them for us?

First: I am actually learning how to drive. Second: I have moved into my own apartment.

Which is the more significant?

If I had to make the best guess, it would be driving.

Why do you consider driving your greater achievement?

It gives me more freedom.

I believe that sometime in the past, you attempted to drive.

Yes, I first attempted it in a truck, because I need the legroom. I am 6 feet, and I sit Indian style. However, I never felt comfortable in the truck. It took a while to get in the right kind of vehicle. It was a suburban, but even then I was reluctant to get behind the wheel. The suburban has a roomy interior, and I can sit Indian style, with one leg extended to the floor. This is all I need for driving.

Alex, at 23 years of age, what led you to begin to drive in earnest?

I always wanted to drive, but I had my reservations. However, I realized that on Shelter Island, I would be isolated and stuck in my apartment, always dependent on someone else to take me somewhere. It's taken a while to overcome both my physical fears and my psychological reluctance.

What induced you to get behind the wheel?

One night, my dad asked me if I wanted to go to the gas station to pick up some snacks. Just out of the blue, he asked me if I wanted to drive. I thought it was a little crazy, since it was nighttime. But, Dad thought that since I had trouble in the mornings when everyone is on the road, it would be better at night, when the roads are empty. Shelter Island is very quiet at night, and the roads are quite empty.

Even though my driving leg was uncomfortable, I made the effort and drove. It irritated me as I drove. But, I was surprised that I drove really well. By the time I got back home, I lay in bed and pondered the experience. I took to driving fairly well and felt pretty good about myself. I considered giving driving a second chance. I began to feel different.

How often do you drive now?

I have been practice driving for a month, almost every day. Two years ago, I took the written test and passed. But, I didn't drive until recently. Back then, I had the attitude of a kid. I didn't realize the benefits of driving. I didn't want to deal with the personal trauma and initial inconvenience.

What helped to bring about the change?

Now that I am older and more mature, I am less apprehensive and have more confidence in myself. I still have to have someone in the car to assist me with directions and give me added assurance. I know someday soon I will be able to drive alone, but only on Shelter Island, where there are no lights, and traffic is not heavy. As for leaving the island, when I drive, I would still have to have someone with me.

When you drive now, how long can you drive for?

I can usually last an hour, but I haven't taken any long-distance trips.

Earlier in the book, you spoke about your sense of direction, which was a major obstacle to driving. How are you handling it now?

Surprisingly, I am much better at it now. I play a lot of video games, and I think this might help. Previously, I had no need to remember streets and directions. Now, with constant driving, I find my sense of direction much improved.

As a driver, how will you handle situations that may cause you great anxiety and panic? For example, let's say you are in a major accident. How would you react?

First, I would find a way to calm down and be comfortable. I would find a way to relieve the stress. I also know that if I remain calm, help will come. As long as I stop the car, I know nothing else will happen. Right now, I am in the beginning stages of driving, and I hope that with more experience and confidence, I will learn to handle these problems. I am in no rush to go for my driver's license. I definitely will, someday. Right now, I am still building confidence and skill.

Please describe what it is like living in your new apartment.

Simply put, when it comes to my apartment, I'm not living fully on my own. I am not paying my own rent or bills. I am just basically living in another house, in a large three-bedroom apartment instead of a basement room in my father's home.

What makes it different?

Well, I am now more independent and can live alone. I am able to transfer the skills of cooking and sleeping overnight with no one nearby.

What helped in the transition?

For one, I am not totally isolated from anyone. I am connected to a very public area, which means I get to meet a lot of people, and if I ever get irritated or bored by myself, I can just walk out the door and say hello. I am just feet away from my father's gas station, which has a grocery store in it. So if I run out of anything, I can just pop in and get what I need.

Have there been any days or nights in which you felt you must return home?

I can't say, as I have only been here 2 weeks. There are some days when some issues build up, and I get anxious. But so far, I haven't gone home yet. If there are problems where I get overwhelmed, Dad says I can always return home. Again, so far, so good.

It looks like you will be here for a while to come; do you expect to pay rent someday?

Hopefully, some day, especially if my book does well and my other writings sell.

How did you get the courage to move out?

I got lonely living in isolation. When my dad mentioned it, I was quick to jump at the opportunity. Besides, it gives me the opportunity to meet people. Now all I have to do is go down to my dad's gas station and grocery store, and I can meet all the people I want.

That's interesting, Alex. Five years ago when we first met, you seemed very shy and introverted—reluctant to meet people.

I guess you can say it is part of my growing maturity and the success I have had with public speaking. I still get a bit nervous, but I seem to hide it pretty well.

Was there apprehension when the move finally came?

I was kind of nervous, but not overwhelmed.

A few months ago, I asked you if you would like to learn to drive by first learning to drive my golf cart. You said, "No!" because of the drawback of having to sit Indian style. Alex, I am wondering how you overcame your need to sit Indian style. What helped you make the change?

Well as I said, now I drive with one leg on the floor and the other one under me. It seems that I am able to tolerate this fairly well.

Alex, would you consider sitting Indian style a form of stimming?

I don't consider it stimming. Rather, it is just the way I sit; it gives me comfort when I sit. As I said earlier, I adapted this sitting posture early, in kindergarten.

So, if it is a habit, do you feel, now that you can make adjustments?

If it is a habit, I am making an adjustment; however, the other part of my comfort is something necessary.

Do you recall earlier in the book when you were in the Department of Motor Vehicles with a friend? You felt anxious and uncomfortable, and instead of flapping your arms for relief, you reverted to simply moving your fingers in a back-and-forth motion. So, you are capable of making adjustments to what is called "stimming."

I guess so, if that is what you call it.

Do you consider this sensitivity you feel sitting Indian style to be part of your Asperger's syndrome, or is it a habit you adopted long ago?

I think it is a combination of both, but I can't say for sure. When I drive, my mind is totally preoccupied, which keeps me from thinking about the need to sit totally Indian style.

Has this element of "preoccupation," absorption, concentration, or whatever you want to call it, occurred with other symptoms of Asperger's, and has it helped you to deal with them better?

Yes.

So do you believe people with Asperger's can make adaptations to stimming as they grow more mature?

Yes, it is not impossible.

Alex, in writing the book, do you feel you have achieved your goal?

"My hope is that you will treat people with Asperger's syndrome as equals and calmly give us more respect and treat us right."

Yes!

ABOUT THE AUTHORS

ALEX OLINKIEWICZ is an accomplished public speaker. He has received rave reviews in his evaluations.

Here are some direct quotes from parents, teachers, and counselors who have watched Alex's YouTube video or attended his speeches and conferences:

"Unbelievable—probably had the greatest impact on my career."

"I learned more about Asperger's here than I have in the last 5 years."

"This is the best workshop I have ever attended."

"Alex is amazing. Alex Olinkiewicz is an inspiration."

RICHARD O'CONNELL, EdD, is a retired school counselor, a New York state Counselor of the Year, and author of two award-winning books: *Motivating Kids to the Max*, a book for parents, available at *www.createspace.com/3177387*; and *The Secrets to Being a Great School Counselor*, a book for counselors, available at *www.createspace.com/3508330*.

Future Horizons is also proud to publish these titles by Dr Temple Grandin

Named Outstanding Literary Work of the Year by the Autism Society of America

These acclaimed books may be purchased directly from www.FHautism.com.

You may also purchase the Dr Temple Grandin Library, a discounted package with many of Temple's most groundbreaking works.